Reconciliation

A User's Manual

Nihil Obstat: John J. O'Flaherty
                  Censor Librorum

Imprimatur: + John M. Sherlock, D.D.
                  Bishop of London

                  June 18, 2001

Imprimi Potest: Richard Thibodeau, C.Ss.R.
                  Provincial, Denver Province
                  The Redemptorists

Reconciliation

A User's Manual

Fr. Michael Prieur

NOVALIS

Liguori

LIGUORI, MISSOURI

© 2002 Novalis, Saint Paul University, Ottawa, Canada

Cover design: Blair Turner
Layout: Christiane Lemire and Caroline Gagnon

Business Office:
Novalis
49 Front Street East, 2nd Floor
Toronto, Ontario, Canada
M5E 1B3

Phone: 1-800-387-7164 or (416) 363-3303
Fax: 1-800-204-4140 or (416) 363-9409
E-mail: cservice@novalis.ca

ISBN 2-89507-166-7

National Library of Canada Catalogue Record: C2001-904102-0

Published in the United States by Liguori Publications
Liguori, Missouri
www.liguori.org
www.catholicbooksonline.com

U.S. ISBN: 0-7648-0838-9

Library of Congress Catalog Card Number:
2001099091

Printed in Canada.

We acknowledge the financial support of the Government of Canada through the Book Publishing Industry Development Program (BPIDP) for our publishing activities.

Contents

Foreword 7
Reconciliation: The Reason for Jesus 9
The Sacrament of Reconciliation is Liturgy 11

The Three "Rites" of Reconciliation
   in the New Ritual of 1974 13

Examining Your Conscience 17
Ten Practical Tips to Help You Examine
   Your Conscience 23
General Readings for Examination
of Conscience 29
– An Opening Prayer 29
– Seek the Lord 29
– The Ten Commandments 30
– The New Law: The Gift of the Holy Spirit 31
– Jesus' Call to Poverty 31
– The Beatitudes 32
– The Three Major Concerns of Jesus 33
– What True Religion Is 33
– Christian Love 34
– Christian Hope 34
– The Precepts of the Church 35
– Theological Virtues 36
– Cardinal Virtues 36
– Spiritual Works of Mercy 37
– Corporal Works of Mercy 37
– Seven Capital Sins 37

Examination of Conscience: A General Guide 39
– For Children 41
– For Teens and Young Adults 43
– For Married People 45

– For People Who Are Single, Separated,
    Divorced or Widowed 49
– For People Who Are Ill 51
– For Older People 53
– For Priests, Religious and Ministers
    of the Church 55
– For Those Who Have Been Away a Long Time
    (Or an Adult Making a First Confession) 59
– For Those Seeking to Identify a Root Problem 63

Examination of Consciousness:
    A New Approach to Preparing for
    Confession 67

How to Celebrate the Sacrament of
Reconciliation 71
– Preparing your confession 71
– When you are with the priest 71
– The prayer of absolution 71
– Summary 74

Prayers of Sorrow to Be Used as
Acts of Contrition 75

The Word of God 81
A – For those who have difficulty loving and forgiving others
B – For those who are discouraged by their weakness and sin
C – For those who need to pass from legalism to commandments as signs of love
D – For those who have recently returned after a long absence
E – For those who need to be reminded of God's great mercy and Fatherly love
F – For those who see that their lives must change

Foreword

It has been about 30 years since the new Rite of Penance was published in 1974. In this time, the way we go to confession has changed dramatically, and many people no longer go at all. And yet, there are still many who continue to celebrate the sacrament and experience peace, consolation and deep healing.

First published in 1978 under the title *Lord, That I May See*, this handbook was aimed at helping people to discover the richness of the "new way" of going to confession and experience the deep forgiveness and healing that the Lord offers through the Sacrament of Reconciliation.

A few well-worn copies of this little handbook remained but people were requesting new ones. We approached Novalis and, with a new editor, Kevin Burns, Father Michael Prieur set out to keep the best parts and to update and add some insights that had been gained over the years.

Reconciliation: A User's Manual will assist both priests and penitents in unlocking the full potential of the Rite, especially the Rite of Reconciliation of Individual Penitents. Too often today we hear the frustrated plea of a penitent: "I want to go but I don't know how," or "I don't know what to say." This guide is meant to be user-friendly, accessible and easily carried home or kept near the place where the sacrament is celebrated. It is meant to help the penitent to prepare and the priest to recommend specific scripture texts and prayers.

Father Prieur offers some valuable suggestions and help for examining one's conscience. The Scriptures, God's Word, are more familiar to people today. It is here that the Spirit of God speaks to many people. Scripture passages are organized according to various circumstances, such as "For those who have difficulty loving and forgiving others" and "For those who see that their lives must change." Whatever you are experiencing in your life, you will find consolation and encouragement here.

This publication will make it possible for more and more people to come to know what the Rite of Penance is meant to be, and will help them experience the joy, peace, forgiveness and healing that the Lord is offering to all who ask for it.

Father Michael O'Brien

Michael O'Brien is a priest of the Diocese of London, Canada. Associate editor of *Lord, That I May See*, he is now pastor of Our Lady Help of Christians, Watford, and St. Matthew's, Alvinston, Ontario.

Reconciliation:
The Reason for Jesus

God the Father sent his Son, Jesus, to our world for one reason: to reconcile us to God and to one another. This happens specifically through the passion, death and resurrection of Jesus, which we call the paschal mystery. This reconciliation is also the primary task of the Holy Spirit, Jesus' first gift to us. Our celebration of this remarkable gift of God, called the Sacrament of Reconciliation, is in need of renewal in our faith-life today. There is no greater way to witness to the saving power of God than by becoming "ambassadors of reconciliation." We do this both in our personal celebrations of the Sacrament of Reconciliation and in our witnessing to the love of God in the world by countless other acts of healing reconciliation.

It is not surprising that the prayer of absolution, proclaimed by the priest when he absolves us in the Sacrament of Reconciliation, is so full of trinitarian and paschal mystery themes. (See page 73 for this prayer.) Young and old look up with eyes of wonder and peace when the priest raises his hand over them and fervently prays this brief prayer. The priest's dismissal, "Go in peace; your sins are forgiven," must surely be some of the most consoling words anyone can hear this side of heaven.

St. Paul reminds us that we become a *new creation* when we are reconciled. (See 2 Corinthians 5:16-17.) The power of the cross of Jesus enables us to experience forgiveness. Our sins are forgiven! Our relationship to God is totally restored. Now we are called to be inclusive and welcoming to everyone simply because Jesus died for all of us sinners, no matter who we are or what we have done. We, like the disciples on the road to Emmaus in the gospel of Luke, are invited to share in a eucharistic meal that truly makes our hearts "burn within us" when we hear Jesus' word and receive his forgiving love. It is through the varied ways of celebrating reconciliation in our Church and in all of creation that we can receive that deep peace, *Shalom*, that addresses the disharmony of our existence and brings us back to wholeness and integrity. There is no greater good news on earth than this reconciliation that Jesus came to bring to us.

The Sacrament of Reconciliation is Liturgy

Most of us, when we go to confession, would not immediately think of this act as "liturgy" (i.e., the official public prayer of the Church). But every celebration of a sacrament *is* truly liturgy. Each sacrament has as its model the paschal mystery. We gather together; we hear the word of God; we prepare ourselves and our gifts to be transformed; we invoke the power of Jesus to act through and with us before the Father in the Spirit; we are truly united with God and each other in a new way; and then we are sent forth as missionaries of the good news to all we meet. The new Rite of Penance (1974) emphasized this whole process by recommending that we read from Scripture at every celebration, even in individual confession to a priest. This rite allows for moments of dialogue with the priest and opportunities to respond to the prayers and blessings given. Our "offering" is our confession of our sins, and the sorrow we manifest, and our desire to experience a new conversion, or change of heart. Christ acts in the powerful words of absolution spoken by the priest, words that bring us forgiveness, healing and peace-filled reconciliation with God and with the

Church. We are sent forth to do an act of penance in the spirit of the new conversion of our hearts. We have experienced "a second baptism after the shipwreck of sin," as Tertullian and St. Jerome liked to say.

The Three "Rites"
of Reconciliation
in the New Ritual of 1974

The Latin root of the word "reconciliation" is *re + con + cilius*. *Con* means "with"; *cilius* means "hair or eyelash": together they mean "to blink." *Re* means again and again. When we blink, we cleanse our eyes so that we can see clearly. When we experience reconciliation, in effect we "blink" in order to cleanse our "spiritual eyes" or our soul so that we can see again with new clarity, harmony and vision.

The *Rite of Penance* includes three different forms:

• The first form is a "Rite of Reconciliation of Individual Penitents," which is the way most of us have experienced confession in our lives as Catholics.

• The second form is the "Rite for Reconciliation of Several Penitents with Individual Confession and Absolution." This is the form used when we have communal celebrations of Reconciliation that are followed by individual confession to a priest. This rite, which is used in many dioceses today, is appropriate when we want to emphasize the communal dimension of sin and forgiveness. It is also very helpful when we want to examine our consciences from a social justice perspective, or to address some deep wounds experienced in the community, such as anger and bitterness around a labour dispute, a local experience of prejudice or bigotry, or a scandal that affects many people in a parish.

• The third form is the "Rite for Reconciliation of Several Penitents with General Confession and Absolution." Although many of us have participated in services of "General Absolution," this form is intended to be used in exceptional circumstances, such as when a large number of penitents is gathered and there are not enough priests to meet with them individually. In such cases, forgiveness is truly given through the absolution by the priest, with the admonition that all serious sins must be confessed individually to a priest before the person receives general absolution again. The reason for this is that serious sins have serious consequences, and the Church must attend to these through the priest. He is the one, for example, who can determine morally the amount of restitution to be made for serious sins of theft.

This user's manual offers help for all three rites, but it focuses primarily on individual confession with a priest in a personal, one-on-one situation. For many reasons this is the ideal way to celebrate the sacrament, since it allows time for a careful articulation of one's sins as well as for the insightful and prudent counsel of a good confessor. It gives people direct access to a priest who is a "physician of the soul," a true specialist in understanding human moral failings, and one who can bring to the penitent the healing "kiss of Christ," as Catherine Doherty, founder of the Madonna House community, calls the Sacrament of Reconciliation.

Examining Your Conscience

When we are preparing to celebrate the Sacrament of Reconciliation, we first "examine our conscience." A healthy reassessment of our understanding of what this means has allowed us to see this whole process in a more responsible and mature way. To help you examine your conscience, here are a few insights that will encourage a more fruitful confession.

Everybody has a conscience

Almost every known culture presents in its religious writings some idea of the reality of conscience. St. Paul points out that even those who have never heard of the Law are led by reason to do what the Law commands (see Romans 2:14). Human beings have a built-in "moral sense" that urges them to do what is good and right and to avoid what is evil and wrong. This inner sense may at times be rather vague, and even far from what Jesus expects, but it is still present in all of us.

Jesus and conscience

Jesus never used the word "conscience"; at least, we do not find it in his statements in the Gospels. He preferred images and metaphors. He referred to what happens in our "hearts." What comes from our hearts is our response to what God is asking us to do in life. Jesus described our hearts – that is, our innermost personal selves – as the seat or source of this moral sense, what we call conscience. Thus, we have good hearts, loving hearts, hearts of flesh, or a change of heart, which refers to a moral conversion. Or we have hard hearts, stubborn hearts, rebellious hearts, or hearts of stone when we refuse to live as God wants us to live. To Jesus, our hearts represent our conscience.

St. Paul and conscience

St. Paul is the great theologian of conscience in the New Testament. When he used the word "conscience," it had several possible meanings. Sometimes it meant "moral judgment" or a reaction to our conduct; sometimes it meant "awareness of responsibility"; and often it signified "witness." When Vatican Council II (1962–65) spoke of the "voice of conscience," it was alluding to this inner voice of the Holy Spirit whispering gentle hints of what God is calling us to do. This voice could be urging us to praise God and our actions when they are good as well as challenging us and making us take responsibility for our actions when we make mistakes or hurt others. Conscience can both praise and chastise.

Is the term "sin" still a valid way of speaking of wrongdoing today?

Absolutely! Our modern times tend to describe moral evil as "improprieties," "misdemeanours," "slip-ups" or "bad manners" in an effort to water down the profound religious dimensions of sin. However, we need to insist on using the word "sin" because doing so forces us to recognize that our relationships are both "horizontal" (i.e., with other people) and "vertical" (with God). One of the best descriptions of sin in the Bible comes after King David had broken at least five of the ten commandments in his sorry escapade with Uriah's wife, Bathsheba. After David had Uriah killed in battle to cover up his own sin, Scripture says, "What David had done displeased the LORD" (2 Samuel 11:27). Here we see God grieving at what his beloved chosen king had done in spite of God's overwhelming goodness to him. Truly, sin hurts our relationship with God as well as with others. Sin separates us from God; reconciliation heals the break.

Perhaps today we do not describe sin in terms that people can understand. Breaking God's commandments and violating Jesus' call to love God and our neighbour are still wrong. But we need reconciliation for many situations, such as the alienation, isolation, anxiety and frustration that fill our frenetic world. Fear of the future, loss of self-esteem, feeling like a slave in an increasingly impersonal and technological world – all these attitudes can be brought to the Sacrament of Reconciliation for healing and a change of heart. They are often symptoms of deeper, sinful attitudes, such as lack of trust in God, the desire to succeed at all costs, or a need to dominate or control others, all of which manifest pride. We need to unearth these modern manifestations of a human-centred approach to life in order to see how God wants us to live. Sin is still very much with us, and we must address it with an honest and humble heart.

Describing conscience in the 21st century

The *Catechism of the Catholic Church* describes conscience as a "judgment of reason whereby the human person recognizes the moral quality of a concrete act that he or she is going to perform, is in the process of performing, or has already completed." (#1778) To this excellent description of conscience we can add another, this time in the first person singular: Conscience is the awareness in my heart of what I have done or not done towards God and my neighbour. These two descriptions stress several key points:

• Our conscience is our personal *reaction* and *evaluation* of all our daily activities and our thoughtful or thoughtless actions.

• Our conscience involves our whole person; it is not simply an activity of our intellect or will.

• Our conscience moves us to praise, thanksgiving, peace and joy when we respond positively to what God asks of us; it is not only a reminder of where we have failed, which has perhaps been over-emphasized in the past.

• Our conscience needs objective laws, demands or norms to which we can respond. Without these models, goals and laws, we easily become totally relative in our approach to life. We also become mediocre, complacent and self-satisfied; *we* become the norm of our activity and we end up fashioning a world according to what we want and not according to what God wants. (This is our greatest challenge in the 21st century.)

• Our conscience needs to grow; all too often, we examine our conscience for our confessions the same way we did when we were children. Yet, like a good musician or athlete, our conscience should become more sensitive, experienced and perceptive to what God is calling us to do as we mature. This kind of growth brings much more joy to our lives as well as a deeper commitment to grow in our Christian integrity.

Ten Practical Tips to Help You Examine Your Conscience

1. Take your time

To look deeply into your heart takes more than a few minutes. Give yourself a few days or a week to prepare your examination of conscience. Let God's light come gradually into each room of your heart.

Then, when you do come to confession, you can spend the time immediately before you celebrate the sacrament summarizing what God has shown you and asking God to help you to be truly sorry for your sins and to lead you to a deep change of heart.

2. Pray, pray, pray!

Only God can change our hearts and truly convert us. But we must let God work and listen intently to him through prayer.

By listening closely to Jesus we ensure that our examinations of conscience are fruitful rather than "in a rut."

One of the most simple and penetrating prayers is the heart-felt repetition of "The Jesus Prayer": "Lord Jesus Christ, Son of the living God, have mercy on me, a sinner." Many people pray this prayer often throughout the day, so that it becomes a part of them.

3. Look at what Jesus has done for you

This is where you should begin your examination of conscience: by remembering that Jesus loves you, calls you, and gives you everything you need to follow his way.

But we do not always listen to Jesus' call. When we realize how much God has done and is doing for us, we become aware of our poor response to him. As you examine your conscience, resolve to listen to the call of Jesus in your daily life.

Just before you confess your sins to the priest, mention a few of God's blessings in your life.

4. Be honest with yourself

Nothing is ever gained by trying to cover up or by evading what God reveals to us about our sinfulness. By showing us how we have sinned, God helps us to grow in his love.

The more the light of Christ shines in our hearts, the more we will see our own sins. This is good. It means that Christ our Light is becoming brighter and brighter within us. Be consoled: the greatest saints saw themselves as the worst sinners.

Finally, if we want to be honest, we must do what St. Francis de Sales recommends: find the motive for our actions or attitudes. We must ask ourselves, for example, *Why am I impatient or angry?* This helps us to get at the root of our problem, which may be one of the capital sins, such as pride or envy.

5. Mention the number of times you have sinned

St. Alphonsus once said that if an elephant walked into our living room, we would know it! (I would add that if it happened more than once, we would remember how many times!) If we have seriously offended God or our brother or sister, we will usually know whether we have done so one or ten times.

How often we commit less serious offences can be an excellent sign or symptom of a deeper tendency or attitude such as pride, jealousy, and so on. Mentioning how often you have sinned can be a great help to your confessor. For example, if you have been impatient a dozen times a day during the past week, then you could try to get at the reason for this. The impatience is only the symptom.

6. Let Scripture be your guide

If you feel that your examinations of conscience usually end with the same problems or sins and if you want to grow in new areas, ask God to let Scripture speak to you in fresh ways.

Listen for words, phrases and themes in the readings at Mass that strike you again and again. This is God preparing you for his call. You may also wish to read the Bible at home or to join a scripture study group to become more familiar with God's word and how it speaks to you.

Bring a scripture passage that is meaningful to you to your confession and concentrate on it with your confessor. It is God's Word calling you to follow him more faithfully.

7. Use three simple words to focus your examination of conscience

Reading the Commandments, the Beatitudes, the Cardinal Virtues or the signs of love of St. Paul (1 Corinthians 13) will reveal how you are responding to God's call. Try using them to examine your conscience. (The above are listed in the readings in the second half of this book.)

Three simple words, each beginning with the same letter, assess our personal response:
– *Family*
– *Friends*
– *Faith*

By expanding on these, you will have an excellent basis for an examination of conscience (see pages 39-66).

8. Know your own "signs of slippage"

Each person has a "faith-response barometer." Rather than committing a serious sin out of the blue, most people gradually slip into sin. A storm seldom comes up in two minutes. Neither does sinning come suddenly.

These signs of slipping usually do not seem serious. But when they occur frequently, they remind us to stop, look and listen. The Lord is calling for a change of heart; sacramental confession is often the way to get there.

Signs of slippage vary with each individual. If we learn to read our own early warning signs, we can avoid a routine approach to our confessions. We must remember that God calls us to new conversion.

9. Review five common "signs of slippage"

1 – Whenever I notice myself being *intolerant* or *impatient* with others, or *failing to love my neighbour as myself*;

2 – Whenever I notice that I am *selfish, manipulative,* or *turning in on myself* through self-pity;

3 – Whenever I let the *fear of the future* weigh me down so much that *I depend on myself more than on God*;

4 – Whenever I find that *I no longer marvel* at the hand of God acting in my life or in the lives of others, or *I no longer rejoice* at a fresh change of heart in myself or others;

5 – Whenever I feel that *the Gospel,* the Good News, *tastes like sawdust* in my mouth. (This can be a special sign for priests and teachers of the faith; it can mean we are not constant in prayer.)

10. Put your trust in God

God made us and knows us better than we know ourselves. St. Augustine says God is also closer to us than we are to ourselves!

God is not a bookkeeper or a grim judge who tallies up our sins. God is a loving Father, waiting for us to answer his call of love to come home. Like the forgiving father in the parable of the Prodigal Son, he waits for us with open arms and rejoices when we return.

The great gift God wants us to experience is "joyful trust," which is a result of being reconciled to him (Romans 5:11). This is the true fruit of forgiveness.

General Readings for Examination of Conscience

As you examine your conscience, you may wish to use one or more of the following readings to guide you.

An Opening Prayer

"Help my soul, mighty Lord; support it, O Father of mankind. Heal it yet again, eternal God, our Judge, strong and powerful, in all its distress. Sin-stained it is, and times there are when I fear for my soul, despite the kindness you have shown me in my life here. Thanks be to you for all those undeserved gifts and mercies. From the memory of these will I take heart, look forward with cheerful trust and gird myself for the way to come." (From the *Exeter Book,* 10th century)

Seek the Lord

"From there you will seek the LORD your God, and you will find him if you search after him with all your heart and soul. In your distress, when all these things have happened to you in time to come, you will return to the LORD your God and heed him. Because the LORD your God is a merciful

God, he will neither abandon you nor destroy you; he will not forget the covenant with your ancestors that he swore to them." (Deuteronomy 4:29-31)

The Ten Commandments

The Ten Commandments, given to Moses by God, set out God's law:

"I am the LORD your God, who brought you out of the land of Egypt, out of the house of slavery; you shall have no other gods before me. You shall not make for yourself an idol, whether in the form of anything that is in heaven above, or that is on the earth beneath, or that is in the water under the earth. You shall not bow down to them or worship them; for I the LORD your God am a jealous God, punishing children for the iniquity of parents, to the third and the fourth generation of those who reject me, but showing steadfast love to the thousandth generation of those who love me and keep my commandments. You shall not make wrongful use of the name of the LORD your God, for the LORD will not acquit anyone who misuses his name. Remember the sabbath day, and keep it holy. Six days you shall labour and do all your work. But the seventh day is a sabbath to the LORD your God; you shall not do any work – you, your son or your daughter, your male or female slave, your livestock, or the alien resident in your towns.

For in six days the Lord made heaven and earth, the sea, and all that is in them, but rested the seventh day; therefore the Lord blessed the sabbath day and consecrated it.

Honour your father and your mother, so that your days may be long in the land that the Lord your God is giving you.

You shall not murder.

You shall not commit adultery.

You shall not steal.

You shall not bear false witness against your neighbour.

You shall not covet your neighbour's house; you shall not covet your neighbour's wife, or male or female slave, or ox, or donkey, or anything that belongs to your neighbour."
(Exodus 20:2-17)

The New Law: The Gift of the Holy Spirit

St. Thomas Aquinas points out that what is specific to the New Law – the law of love – is the gift of the Holy Spirit. This is how St. Paul puts it:

"And because you are children, God has sent the Spirit of his Son into our hearts, crying, 'Abba! Father!' So you are no longer a slave but a child, and if a child then also an heir, through God."
(Galatians 4:6-7)

Jesus' Call to Poverty

As he was setting out on a journey, a man ran up and knelt before him, and asked him, "Good

Teacher, what must I do to inherit eternal life?" Jesus said to him, "Why do you call me good? No one is good but God alone. You know the commandments: You shall not murder; You shall not commit adultery; You shall not steal; You shall not bear false witness; You shall not defraud; Honour your father and mother." He said to him, "Teacher, I have kept all these since my youth." Jesus, looking at him, loved him and said, "You lack one thing; go, sell what you own, and give the money to the poor, and you will have treasure in heaven; then come, follow me." When he heard this, he was shocked and went away grieving, for he had many possessions." (Mark 10:17-22)

The Beatitudes

When Jesus saw the crowds, he went up the mountain; and after he sat down, his disciples came to him. Then he began to speak, and taught them, saying:

"Blessed are the poor in spirit, for theirs is the kingdom of heaven.

Blessed are those who mourn, for they will be comforted.

Blessed are the meek, for they will inherit the earth.

Blessed are those who hunger and thirst for righteousness, for they will be filled.

Blessed are the merciful, for they will receive mercy.

Blessed are the pure in heart, for they will see God.

Blessed are the peacemakers, for they will be called children of God.

Blessed are those who are persecuted for righteousness' sake, for theirs is the kingdom of heaven.

Blessed are you when people revile you and persecute you and utter all kinds of evil against you falsely on my account. Rejoice and be glad, for your reward is great in heaven, for in the same way they persecuted the prophets who were before you." (Matthew 5:1-12) (See also Matthew 5:13-48; 6:1-34; 7:1-29.)

The Three Major Concerns of Jesus

"Woe to you, scribes and Pharisees, hypocrites! For you tithe mint, dill, and cummin, and have neglected the weightier matters of the law: justice and mercy and faith. It is these you ought to have practised without neglecting the others. You blind guides! You strain out a gnat but swallow a camel!" (Matthew 23:23-24)

What True Religion Is

"If any think they are religious, and do not bridle their tongues but deceive their hearts, their religion is worthless. Religion that is pure and undefiled before God, the Father, is this:

to care for orphans and widows in their distress, and to keep oneself unstained by the world." (James 1:26-27)

Christian Love

"Love is patient; love is kind; love is not envious or boastful or arrogant or rude. It does not insist on its own way; it is not irritable or resentful; it does not rejoice in wrongdoing, but rejoices in the truth. It bears all things, believes all things, hopes all things, endures all things." (1 Corinthians 13:4-7)

Christian Hope

"More than that, I regard everything as loss because of the surpassing value of knowing Christ Jesus my Lord. For his sake I have suffered the loss of all things, and I regard them as rubbish, in order that I may gain Christ and be found in him, not having a righteousness of my own that comes from the law, but one that comes through faith in Christ, the righteousness from God based on faith. I want to know Christ and the power of his resurrection and the sharing of his sufferings by becoming like him in his death, if somehow I may attain the resurrection from the dead. Not that I have already obtained this or have already reached the goal; but I press on to make it my own, because Christ Jesus has made me his own." (Philippians 3:8-12)

The Precepts of the Church

From time to time the Church has listed certain specific duties of Catholics. In the *Catechism of the Catholic Church* these are outlined as follows:

The precepts of the Church are set in the context of a moral life bound to and nourished by liturgical life. The obligatory character of these positive laws decreed by the pastoral authorities is meant to guarantee to the faithful the indispensable minimum in the spirit of prayer and moral effort, in the growth of love of God and neighbour.

The first precept ("You shall attend Mass on Sundays and holy days of obligation") requires the faithful to participate in the eucharistic celebration when the Christian community gathers together on the day commemorating the Resurrection of the Lord.

The second precept ("You shall confess your sins at least once a year") ensures preparation for the Eucharist when we are conscious of serious sin by the reception of the sacrament of reconciliation, which continues Baptism's work of conversion and forgiveness.

The third precept ("You shall humbly receive your Creator in Holy Communion at least during the Easter season") guarantees as a minimum the reception of the Lord's Body and Blood in connection with the Paschal feasts, the origin and centre of the Christian liturgy.

The fourth precept ("You shall keep the holy days of obligation") completes the Sunday observance by participation in the principal liturgical feasts which honour the mysteries of the Lord, the Virgin Mary and the Saints.

The fifth precept ("You shall observe the prescribed days of fasting and abstinence") ensures the times of asceticism and penance which prepare us for the liturgical feasts; they help us acquire mastery over our instincts and freedom of heart.

The faithful also have the duty of providing for the material needs of the Church, each according to his [or her] abilities. (#2041–2043)

Theological Virtues

(the virtues having God as their direct object)
– Faith, or belief in God's infallible teaching
– Hope, or confidence in divine assistance
– Charity, or love of the Supreme God

Cardinal Virtues

(the four principal moral virtues)
– Prudence
– Justice
– Temperance
– Fortitude

Spiritual Works of Mercy

(Works of spiritual assistance, motivated by love of God and neighbour, to persons in need)
– counselling the doubtful
– instructing the ignorant
– admonishing sinners
– comforting the afflicted
– forgiving offences
– bearing wrongs patiently
– praying for the living and the dead

Corporal Works of Mercy

– feeding the hungry
– giving drink to the thirsty
– clothing the naked
– visiting the imprisoned
– sheltering the homeless
– visiting the sick
– burying the dead

Seven Capital Sins

(moral faults which, if habitual, give rise to many more sins)
– pride
– covetousness
– lust
– anger
– gluttony
– envy
– sloth

Examination of Conscience:
A General Guide

For most of us it is impossible to include all our sins and failures when we examine our consciences. Most examinations of conscience can be reduced to two key questions:

1) In what major ways have I displeased God?

2) Which of my actions are getting in the way of my love for God and my neighbour?

Often the problem is that we continue to examine our consciences the way we were taught as children. We have not allowed the light of God to open new areas of growth in us. Keep this in mind as we look at specific examinations of conscience below. They are neither all-inclusive nor final. They are springboards for pondering.

Pray that God's warm light will brighten your heart and show you new ways of knowing his loving forgiveness and his call to grow.

Before celebrating the Sacrament of Reconciliation, consider the following questions:

a) What is my attitude towards the Sacrament of Reconciliation?

– Do I sincerely want to be set free from sin, to turn again to God, to begin a new life, and to enter into a deeper relationship with God?

– Or do I look on the sacrament as a burden, to be undertaken as seldom as possible?

(Sacraments are gifts of God, not burdens. Sacraments are for the weak, not the strong. Finally, God does not need the sacraments: *we* do.)

b) Did I forget to mention, or deliberately conceal, any serious sins in past confessions?

c) Did I perform the penance I was given? Did I make reparation for any injury to others? Have I tried to lead a better life in keeping with the Gospel, as I had resolved to do?

For Children

Prayer

Dear Father in Heaven, I am coming to you to tell you my sins and to receive your forgiveness. Help me to be honest and sincere. Help me to be truly sorry for the ways I have offended you. Fill me with your love and your peace so that I may love you more. I ask this in the name of Jesus, my Brother and my Friend. Amen.

Areas of Concern

Family (and School)

• What are *the things at home* that I am doing or not doing that hurt or upset my mother and father or my brothers and sisters? (Being selfish, fighting, being unkind, disobeying, not going to bed when I am told, etc.)

• Do I show *respect* to my parents?

• Do I try to be *helpful* and *cheerful* at home?

• Are my *teachers* ever *displeased* with me? Why? (Talking in class, not doing my work, not listening to instructions, etc.)

Friends

- Do I *help* my classmates when they need it?

- Do I *play fair* at recess? Do I treat others with *respect* in the schoolyard?

- What actions of mine *hurt* my friends? (Being mean, fighting, bullying, making fun of people, etc.)

- Do I *share* my things with my friends?

- Do I *listen* to them when they are sad or upset?

Faith

- Do I *thank* God every day for the good things he does for me?

- Do I *say I am sorry* when I offend God?

Two tips

1) If you have done something that is very serious, then tell the priest how many times it happened. Otherwise, choose the one thing that is giving you the most trouble and ask God and the priest for special help in this area.

2) It is good to try to tell *why* you acted the way you did. For example, "I was fighting with my sister at home because she gets more attention from my dad and I feel left out." Finding the reason for your actions will help you deepen your conscience as you grow older.

For Teens and Young Adults

Prayer

Lord Jesus Christ, you have called us to follow your way. But often we prefer our own way. So we displease you and wander from your truth. Help us to know your love better, to see our sins clearly, and to seek your forgiveness honestly and humbly in this Sacrament of Reconciliation. I ask this in your name. Amen.

Areas of Concern

Family

- Do I *communicate* with my parents and understand their point of view?

- Do I *thank* them for what they do for me?

- Do I have any *main fault* that disrupts the family? (e.g., jealousy, laziness, rudeness, etc.)

- Do I *apologize* and *forgive* quickly?

- Am I *generous and kind* with the other members of the family?

Friends

- Am I *kind* to my friends?

- Do I *help* people in need?

- Am I *too focused on myself?*

- Do I *respect* my girlfriend/boyfriend and avoid sexual situations?

- Do I *respect my body* by avoiding alcohol and drugs, by eating healthy foods and by exercising?

- Do I treat my friends with *care*?

- Am I *responsible* at school, at work, and in the groups to which I belong?

Faith

- Do I ask God to help me be more *faithful, hopeful and loving*?

- Do I go to Mass *humbly* and hungering to meet the Lord in the Eucharist?

- Do I *listen* to God's Word at Mass?

- Do I *thank God* in prayer each day?

- Do I try to *deepen my faith,* even when my life is confusing?

For Married People

Prayer

Father in Heaven, you have called me to do your will through the covenant of marriage. Send your Spirit more into my heart as I approach the Sacrament of Reconciliation. Help me to see with your light the ways that I am not being faithful to this covenant. Fill me with your deep peace, mercy and forgiveness, and help me to grow. All this I ask through Jesus Christ, my Lord and Healer. Amen.

Areas of Concern

Family

- Do I *communicate* in a positive and healthy way with my spouse and my children?

- Do I *apologize* and *forgive* quickly?

- Am I *selfish* or *demanding* at home?

- Am I sexually *faithful* to my spouse?

- Do I allow for *individuality* in my family?

- Do I *respect* the Church's teachings on family planning?

- Does any *predominant attitude* or *fault* of mine disrupt my home?

- Am I doing *all I can* to raise my children in the faith of the Roman Catholic Church?

Friends

- Am I *truthful* and *honest* in all I say and do?

- Am I *at peace* with everyone?

- Do I *treat people* with respect, avoiding inappropriate sexual behaviour?

- Do I *bring out the best* in the people I meet?

- If I am in a position of leadership or management, do I strive to *be just* to those who work for me?

- Have I done *violence to others* by damaging their life or health, reputation, honour or material possessions?

- Do I *share* my gifts with the poor, the sick, the elderly, the lonely, strangers, or people of other races?

- Have I *respected God's gifts* through my actions? (e.g., eating healthily, drinking moderately, giving money and time to charitable organizations, spending money responsibly, etc.)

- Do I strive to work for *social justice*?

- Do I respect *the environment*? Do I teach my children to value the goods of the earth?

Faith

- Do I *listen* to the Lord in prayer?

- Do I put *my faith and trust* in God alone, especially in times of temptation?

- Do I *attend Mass* humbly, yearning for God's word and life-giving Food?

- Am I *striving to know more* about my faith, my Church, my relationship with God?

- Do I willingly and gladly *stand up for my faith?*

- Do I use *the name of Jesus* with love and respect?

For People Who Are Single, Separated, Divorced or Widowed

Prayer

Lord Jesus, you always showed compassion for those who suffered in any way. At times I feel so alone and in need of support and love. Pour your healing Spirit into my heart so that I may know your mercy and loving kindness in a new way. I make this prayer through your most holy Name, Jesus my Saviour. Amen.

Areas of Concern

Family

- Do I work at *relationships* with my family, even when there is tension between us?

- Am I *at peace* with my siblings, my children, and my extended family?

- Do I *speak positively* about my siblings, my children, my former spouse?

- Have I allowed myself to *grieve adequately* for my deceased spouse?

Friends

- Do I give some of my *extra time* to meet the needs of those around me?

- Am I able to *feel positive* about my life as a single person?

- Do I *thank God* each day for the blessings I receive?

- Am I *quick to respond* to the needs of others?

- Do I *take responsibility* for my actions rather than blaming others?

- Do I *reach out to others* in a healthy way when I feel lonely?

Faith

- Am I striving to *live chastely*?

- Do I have a *positive attitude* towards myself?

- Do I give ample time each day to go deeper into *God's word*?

For People Who Are Ill

Prayer

Merciful Father in Heaven, I come to you weighed down by my illness and my sinfulness. Send your Spirit of consolation and healing into my heart as I approach the Sacrament of Reconciliation. Grant me the gifts of forgiveness, peace and joyful trust. This I ask in the name of Jesus Christ, my Saviour and Healer. Amen.

Areas of Concern

Family

- Do I *appreciate* the people who look after me and visit me? Do I let them know it?

- Do I give a *good Christian example* to others?

- Do I *apologize and forgive* quickly?

- Do I *contribute* to the life of my family as much as I can?

Friends

- Am I *thoughtful of my friends* and attentive to others who are ill?

- Am I *sorry* for the ways I have sinned against God and others?

• How do I *show* that I am sorry for my sins towards others?

Faith

• Do I *trust* God's goodness and providence, even in times of stress and illness?

• Do I *try not to give in* to despair or to other negative thoughts and feelings?

• Do I use my quiet moments to *reflect* on life and to pray to God?

• Do I *accept* my illness and pain and know that Jesus, who suffered and died for us, is always with me?

• Do I *pray for* those who are also suffering from illness, loneliness, lack of faith, poverty or injustice?

• Do I *live by faith,* confident that my gifts are important to the life of the Church?

For Older People

Prayer

Our Father in Heaven, I come to you seeking your mercy and love in the Sacrament of Reconciliation. Fill me with a deeper faith and trust in you. Help me to know even more the depths of your forgiveness. I ask you to grant this in the name of your Son, Jesus Christ, who lives and reigns forever. Amen.

Areas of Concern

Family

- Am I *at peace* with all my family? Do I raise issues in a positive, caring way?

- Do I *apologize and forgive* quickly?

- Am I *open to seeing the good* in everyone?

- Do I have any *predominant attitude or fault* that still tends to weigh me down?

Friends

- Do I *try to encourage* others through my experience rather than coming across as a "know-it-all"?

- Am I *open to new ideas* and ways of doing things?

- Do I *try to listen* to those around me and to learn from them?

- Do I *give to the poor* at home or in other parts of the world?

Faith

- Have I increased the amount of time I spend in *prayer*, thanking God for all he has done for me?

- Do I *pray* for deeper faith, greater trust, and a yearning love for God above all?

- Do I *read Sacred Scripture* regularly?

- Do I try to *pass on the wisdom* of my Christian and Catholic faith to others?

For Priests, Religious and Ministers of the Church

Prayer

Lord Jesus Christ, you called me to follow in your footsteps. But I often wander from your path into sinfulness. Send your healing Spirit into my heart. Call me back to your service. Show me your forgiveness and give me the gifts of peace and joyful trust as I approach the Sacrament of Reconciliation. This I ask through your name, you who live and reign forever. Amen.

Prayer for Priests (by Karl Rahner, S.J.)[1]

O my God, I, your anointed and ordained priest, the representative of holy Church – I am a poor sinner and no better than those before whom I am meant to walk as a good shepherd on the paths of salvation. How great a gulf there is between what I am and should be as a priest and what I am as a poor sinner! And how this disparity weighs heavily upon me! How am I to confess it, how destroy the false appearance and the lie which spread around the truth of my priesthood by my guilt! I cannot kneel down before my parishioners to beg them to forgive

---

1. From Karl Rahner, S.J., "Forgotten Truths Concerning Penance," in *Theological Investigations* (London: Darton, Longman & Todd, 1963), Vol. 2, p. 152.

me my guilt towards them, so that God in heaven may forgive me. And, therefore, I confess at least to another priest, to my own brother – in the place of God and God's holy congregation whom I have offended – my fault, my grievous fault....

Do not take me for an exalted saint but regard me rather as what I am through my guilt: a poor sinner. Through this Confession, by showing myself before the Church, and thereby before all against whom I have sinned to be far from what I should be and seem to be, I can hope that God, by the love of his Spirit Whom he bestows, will also place me again where he has placed me by Ordination. By the fact that I show my fetters, he relieves me of them.

Areas of Concern

Family

- Do I *respect my parents*?

- Do I *look after them* as much as I am able?

- Do I *lean on my "position"* in dealing with my family?

- Do I *apologize and forgive* readily?

- Do I *pray frequently* for my parents, siblings, nieces and nephews, and especially for my parish family?

- Do I *support* the members of my religious community in a positive way even if I do not live with them?

Friends

- Do I *reach out* to my fellow priests and religious and offer help when they need it?

- Am I *concerned for God's poor,* rather than simply seeing them as part of my job?

- Am I *positive and supportive* in my observations of the Church, of my bishop, of my pastor or superior?

- Do I *marvel at God's action* in my ministry?

- Am I *open and unselfish* in my friendships?

- Am I striving to have a *deep social conscience?*

- Do I live out my vow of *chastity* or the gift of *celibacy* as I have been called to do?

- Do I see my *sexuality* as an important and healthy part of who I am, and commit this gift to the service of the Lord?

Faith

- Am I *faithful in daily prayer,* both in the Liturgy of the Hours and alone with the Lord?

- Am I constantly *trying to renew* my understanding of the faith, of Sacred Scripture, of theology, and of modern culture?

- Am I *becoming poorer in spirit* rather than acquiring earthly riches?

• Is the *Gospel* truly "Good News" in my ministry?

• Do I *seek regular spiritual direction?* Is the Sacrament of Reconciliation a regular source of healing in my life?

• Do I spend adequate time *praying and reading* to prepare for my preaching?

• Do I plan *regular days of prayer* and an annual retreat to refuel my priestly zeal?

For Those Who Have Been Away a Long Time

(or an Adult Making a First Confession)

Prayer for Those Who Have Been Away a Long Time

Merciful Father in Heaven, I come to you as your lost sheep who has been wandering for a long time. I am weary and tired. I am trembling and afraid. I have done what is displeasing to you. Forgive me, for I have sinned. Send me your Spirit of healing and peace. Take away the fear that is in my heart so that I may confess to you humbly and sincerely. Through this Sacrament may I be reconciled once more to your Church. All this I ask through your Son, Jesus Christ, who lives forever and ever. Amen.

Prayer for an Adult Making a First Confession

Father in Heaven, I come to you seeking your mercy and forgiveness. Through my sins I have displeased you and wandered from your way. Send me your healing Spirit. Take away any fear or anxiety in my heart as I approach this Sacrament of Reconciliation for the first time. Help me to see myself as you see me. Grant me the grace to make a good confession and above all to know your loving kindness. All this I ask in the name of Jesus Christ, my Lord and Redeemer. Amen.

General Questions

- Are there any *major* or *serious* ways that I have sinned against God or my neighbour or

  – against God's commandments?

  – against Jesus' call of love?

  – against the responsibilities of my state in life?

- Do I have any recurring *attitude* or *fault* that is continually weighing me down? (e.g., pride, envy, selfishness, prejudice, anger, hatred, inappropriate sexual behaviour, injustice, lack of forgiveness.) How can I overcome this?

Specific Questions

Family

- Do I *love* the members of my family the way Jesus wants me to?

- Do I *sacrifice* my own desires for the good of others in the family?

- Do I try *to communicate* in a positive and healthy way with my spouse and my children?

- Do I *respect* the Church's teachings on family planning?

Friends

- Am I *at peace* with my friends?

- Am I truly *honest* at work and in all I do?

- Do I try to see *Christ* in the people around me?

- Do I try to make some *sacrifices* for God's poor, at home or in other parts of the world?

Faith

- Do I practise my faith *regularly* and *willingly?*

- Do I *pray* each day, alone and with my family?

- Do I *thank* God often for his many great gifts?

- Am I deepening *my knowledge* of my faith?

For Those Seeking to Identify a Root Problem

Prayer

Lord Jesus Christ, I am coming to you to see more clearly your call in my life. Send your Spirit of discernment into my heart so that I may be able to grow in understanding and love. Let your healing forgiveness bring me a deeper peace. This I ask in your name. Amen.

Specific Statements that May Lead to a "Root Difficulty"

(Attitudinal Concern)

People today often mention the following attitudes that colour their whole approach to life. If you are trying to grow in self-understanding of the possible roots of a recurring attitude, fear or tendency, read over this list and think about which ones apply to you.[2] During your confession, talk to the priest about one or two of these statements and ask for forgiveness, healing or help with further discernment.

---

2. These statements are adapted from Michael Scanlan, T.O.R., *The Power in Penance* (Notre Dame, IN: Ave Maria Press, 1972), pp. 32-34.

• I really think I am better than others so I treat them as inferior.

• I resent _____'s success because I had to work so hard for my own.

• I don't believe I am lovable: therefore I keep everyone away from me by being aggressive.

• Whatever I do leads to sin.

• I resent _____ being more popular than I.

• I lose control of myself when I drink alcohol.

• I've never forgiven _____.

• Rage overcomes me whenever _____ _____ tells me to do something.

• I'm afraid people might find out that I'm a phony.

• I'm angry at God for the situation he puts me in.

• I don't believe God loves me; he judges and punishes.

• I can't stand people doing things for me.

• I enjoy conquering _____.

• I think only of myself.

• I like nurturing my anger against _____ _____.

• I have to prove I'm better than _____
_____ is.

• I'm terribly afraid of being a failure.

Here are different ways to look at these attitudes. They can be a first step in figuring out root problems.

• You feel persecuted and you're fighting back.

• You don't trust anyone.

• You interpret these situations to gain pity for yourself.

• You are too afraid of what others will say about you.

• You want to punish yourself.

• You have given away your freedom to this thing.

• You don't believe you can be forgiven.

• You resent children.

• You feel cheated by your vows.

• You are afraid of what God might ask you to do if you changed.

• You don't want to rely on anyone else, even God.

• You seek excuses to escape your responsibilities.

• You want the credit and glory to go to yourself first.

• You want the power of money and respect more than you want God.

• You feel powerless whenever _____ comes upon you.

Examination of Consciousness: A New Approach to Preparing for Confession

The examination of conscience works for many people. Others, however, are looking for a different, more fruitful way to prepare for confession. Both priests and lay people find a practice called the "examination of consciousness" to be very helpful.

It is called an "examination of consciousness" (rather than "conscience") because the method does not concentrate on any specific thought, word or deed that we have committed. Rather, it concentrates on allowing our inner hearts to remember and to ponder – to "savour" – the inner attitudes, feelings or movements of the heart of the preceding 24 hours, which we perhaps did not have time to dwell upon when they occurred.

This takes about five to ten minutes, but it can certainly go on longer. The important thing is to try to do this *every day* and *at the same time*.

The effects of this practice will not appear on the first day. But after a week or so, many people have indicated the following good results:

– a deeper peace within them;

– a greater awareness of God's gifts in other people;

– a greater awareness of God's hand in their own lives;

– a yearning to praise and thank God more;

– a deeper sorrow for their sins and for their lack of response to God.

This approach emphasizes what God is doing in us and in those around us and helps us prepare for the Sacrament of Reconciliation. Unlike former practices of examination of conscience, which after an initial prayer to the Holy Spirit usually jumped right into confession of one's sins and failures, this process invites us to reflect on God's action in and around us and our response (positive or negative) to God's call before we celebrate the sacrament.

Five Daily Steps

1. Calm down

– Set a regular time each day.

– Get apart from everyone: in a room alone, walking outside, in a church or chapel, etc.

– Get comfortable with God: have a cup of tea or a glass of wine, relax, listen and feel everything around you.

– Don't rush; it is important to slow down if you are to hear the voice of the Lord.

2. Look for the "finger of God" in your day

– Look back over the past 24 hours; try to see where God manifested himself to you (for example, in an encouraging word, a bright smile, a "feeling" of praise, gratitude, sorrow, even emptiness or yearning).

– Recall and savour anything that happened to you that you were not able to reflect on at the time.

– Praise, thank, marvel at, or yearn for God out of this experience of reflection.

3. Examine your response to God's call

– Look at your response to the above situations.

– How have you responded to what God has done for you today?

– If your daily worries, distractions, fears, selfishness, pettiness, etc., interfered with a strong response, bring all this to God.

4. Express sorrow

– Expressing sorrow should arise spontaneously after you examine your response to God's call.

– This sorrow should be true sorrow, not selfpity. True sorrow comes from not living up to the call and expectations *of God*; self-pity comes from failing to live up to *your own* expectations. Sorrow turns our faces towards God; self-pity turns our faces towards ourselves.

5. Resolve to do better

– Christians are called not to wallow in sorrow but to start over again, to trust God, and to keep going, confident that the power of Jesus' death and resurrection has overcome all sin.

– Jesus calls us *out* of our sin. This is the Good News of our salvation.

– Offer a simple resolution, prayer of trust or firm conviction on how you will act the next time such a situation occurs.

– Pray a prayer of praise and thanksgiving to God and to Mary, who intercedes for us.

St. Teresa of Avila used to say that people could judge their spiritual status by how quickly they got up after a fall. An Irish proverb says, "Heaven is full of people who started over again, often." Using this examination of consciousness every day can help you to see God's action more clearly in your life, and to respond more readily to God's constant call to life and to growth.

How to Celebrate the Sacrament of Reconciliation

Preparing your confession

– Pray to the Holy Spirit for self-knowledge and the humility to be totally honest.

– Listen to whatever strikes you from the Word of God at church or in your personal reading; use this "word" to help you with your examination of conscience; then bring this "word" to confession with you.

– Ask God to fill you with true sorrow for your sins because they have offended God, who is so good to you, as well as other people in your life.

– Pray for the conversion of heart and reconciliation that are necessary for forgiveness.

When you are with the priest

– You may kneel or sit depending on your preference and the room.

– Begin with the sign of the cross, then say, "Forgive me, Father, for I have sinned" (or similar words).

– Say how long it has been since your last confession and what your state in life is (married, single, etc.).

– The priest will welcome you and say a brief prayer, such as "May the Lord take away any fears and anxieties and fill you with trust so that you can make a good confession."

– Now you can read one or two lines from the Word of God that struck you during the past week or so (the priest can also read from Scripture if he chooses).

– It is good to mention at this point a few blessings you have received from God.

– Confess your sins openly and candidly, especially any serious sins along with the number of times each was committed, and any circumstances surrounding them.

– You may also confess what is bothering you, such as anxieties and fears; these often can lead to an attitude of heart that needs healing from God.

– Then listen to the priest's advice and respond to any questions he may ask to help you in your conversion of heart; you are also free to ask any question of the priest to help you grow in your life of faith.

– The priest will then ask you to do an act of "satisfaction" or penance for your sins, such as reading from Scripture, doing an act of mercy, saying a prayer, etc.

– The priest will ask you to say out loud or in your heart some act of contrition (sorrow) either in your own words or one you have learned by heart. (See pages 75-80 for a selection of acts of contrition.)

The prayer of absolution

The priest will then pray the prayer of absolution:

God, the Father of Mercies,
through the death and resurrection of his Son
has reconciled the world to himself
and sent the Holy Spirit among us
for the forgiveness of sins;
through the ministry of the Church
may God give you pardon and peace,
and I absolve you from your sins
in the name of the Father, +
and of the Son,
and of the Holy Spirit.

You answer: "Amen."

The priest will end with a short prayer of dismissal, such as "The Lord has freed you from your sins. Go in peace."

After confession

You may wish to remain in the church to do the act of satisfaction the priest asked of you.

Summary

1. Pray for God's help.
2. Listen to Holy Scripture.
3. Examine your conscience.
4. Present yourself to the priest with an opening prayer and introduction.
5. The priest says his opening prayer.
6. Read from Scripture briefly.
7. Name some blessings.
8. Confess your sins.
9. Listen to the priest's advice.
10. Listen for your "penance."
11. Pray your act of contrition.
12. Listen to the prayer of absolution.
13. Respond with "Amen."
14. Listen to the priest's final dismissal.
15. Do your "penance" ("act of satisfaction").

Prayers of Sorrow to Be Used as Acts of Contrition

From the International Committee on English, Rite of Penance, Roman Ritual (P-1 to P-9)

P-1

My God,
I am sorry for my sins with all my heart.
In choosing to do wrong
and failing to do good,
I have sinned against you
whom I should love above all things.
I firmly intend, with your help,
to do penance,
to sin no more,
and to avoid whatever leads me to sin.
Our Saviour Jesus Christ
suffered and died for us.
In his name, my God, have mercy.

P-2

> Remember, Lord, your compassion and mercy
>> which you showed long ago.
> Do not recall the sins and failings of my youth.
> In your mercy remember me, Lord, because
>> of your goodness.

Psalm 25:6-7

P-3

> Wash me from my guilt
> and cleanse me of my sin.
> I acknowledge my offense;
> my sin is before me always.

Psalm 50:4-5

P-4

> Father of mercy,
> like the prodigal son
> I return to you and say:
> "I have sinned against you
> and am no longer worthy to be called
>> your son."
> Christ Jesus, Saviour of the world,
> I pray with the repentant thief
> to whom you promised paradise:
> "Lord, remember me in your kingdom."
> Holy Spirit, fountain of love,
> I call on you with trust:
> "Purify my heart,
> and help me to walk as a child of the light."

P-5

Lord Jesus,
you opened the eyes of the blind,
healed the sick,
forgave the sinful woman,
and after Peter's denial confirmed him in
    your love.
Listen to my prayer:
forgive all my sins,
renew your love in my heart,
help me to live in perfect unity with my
    fellow Christians
that I may proclaim your saving power to
    all the world.

P-6

Lord Jesus,
you chose to be called the friend of sinners.
By your saving death and resurrection
free me from my sins.
May your peace take root in my heart
and bring forth a harvest
of love, holiness, and truth.

P-7

Lord Jesus Christ,
you are the Lamb of God;
you take away the sins of the world.
Through the grace of the Holy Spirit
restore me to friendship with your Father,
cleanse me from every stain of sin

in the blood you shed for me,
and raise me to new life
for the glory of your name.

P-8

Lord God,
in your goodness have mercy on me:
do not look on my sins,
but take away all my guilt.
Create in me a clean heart
and renew within me an upright spirit.

P-9 – *The Jesus Prayer*

Lord Jesus Christ, Son of the living God,
have mercy on me, a sinner.

For Children

From William J. Freburger and James E. Hass,
The Forgiving Christ: A Book of Penitential
Celebrations, *Notre Dame, IN: Ave Maria Press,*
1977.

(P-10 to P-15)

P-10

I am sorry, Lord, that I was not kind to others.
I will ask those I have hurt to forgive me. I ask
You, Lord Jesus, to forgive me. I want to be your
friend again.

P-11

O my God, I have sinned.
I disobeyed you and hurt others.
I am sorry, Lord, forgive me.
I know you love me.
And I want to love you more.

P-12

Father, all that I have, you have given me.
Your Son, Jesus Christ, died to give me
    new life.
I am sorry for having refused your gifts.
I ask you to give me another chance.
Help me to fight the good fight,
to run the race as a true believer,
and to gain the prize that you have prepared
for all those who persevere in the faith.

P-13

Your yoke, O Lord, is easy
and your burden is light,
and still I have sinned
against you and my neighbour.
Forgive me, O Lord.

P-14

My God, I believe that You are the one God. I believe that Your Son, Jesus Christ, became man and died for our sins. I believe that He will come again to judge the living and the dead.

My God, I rely on Your power and mercy to obtain forgiveness of my sins. I rely on your gracious help in this life, so that You will call me to Your Kingdom in the next life.

My God, I love you with my entire being. I wish to direct all my energies to living for You and serving You in Your Church and this world. Amen.

P-15

O my God, I am sorry for my sins with all my heart. In choosing to do wrong and failing to do good, I have sinned against you whom I should love above all things. I firmly intend, with your help, to do penance, to sin no more, and to avoid whatever leads me to sin.

Our Saviour Jesus Christ suffered and died for us. In his name, God have mercy.

The Word of God

Section A

For those who have difficulty loving and forgiving others

John 15:9-17   A-1
I am giving you these commands so that you may love one another.

1 Corinthians 12:31–13:13   A-2
Faith, hope, and love abide, these three; and the greatest of these is love.

1 John 2:3-11   A-3
Whoever loves a brother or sister lives in the light.

1 John 4:11-18   A-4
If we love one another God lives in us.

James 3:1-10   A-5
No one can tame the tongue.

Psalm 32   A-6
Psalm 51   A-7
Psalm 103   A-8
Psalm 145   A-9
Psalm 104   A-10

I am giving you these commands so that you may love one another.

As the Father has loved me, so I have loved you; abide in my love. If you keep my commandments, you will abide in my love, just as I have kept my Father's commandments and abide in his love. I have said these things to you so that my joy may be in you, and that your joy may be complete. "This is my commandment, that you love one another as I have loved you. No one has greater love than this, to lay down one's life for one's friends. You are my friends if you do what I command you. I do not call you servants any longer, because the servant does not know what the master is doing; but I have called you friends, because I have made known to you everything that I have heard from my Father. You did not choose me but I chose you. And I appointed you to go and bear fruit, fruit that will last, so that the Father will give you whatever you ask him in my name. I am giving you these commands so that you may love one another.

1 Corinthians 12:31–13:13   A-2

Faith, hope, and love abide, these three; and the greatest of these is love.

But strive for the greater gifts. And I will show you a still more excellent way.

If I speak in the tongues of mortals and of angels, but do not have love, I am a noisy gong or a clanging cymbal. And if I have prophetic powers, and understand all mysteries and all knowledge, and if I have all faith, so as to remove mountains, but do not have love, I am nothing. If I give away all my possessions, and if I hand over my body so that I may boast, but do not have love, I gain nothing. Love is patient; love is kind; love is not envious or boastful or arrogant or rude. It does not insist on its own way; it is not irritable or resentful; it does not rejoice in wrongdoing, but rejoices in the truth. It bears all things, believes all things, hopes all things, endures all things. Love never ends. But as for prophecies, they will come to an end; as for tongues, they will cease; as for knowledge, it will come to an end. For we know only in part, and we prophesy only in part; but when the complete comes, the partial will come to an end. When I was a child, I spoke like a child, I thought like a child, I reasoned like a child; when I became an adult, I put an end to childish ways. For now we see in a mirror, dimly, but then we will see face to face. Now I know only in part; then I will know fully, even as I have been fully known. And now faith, hope, and love abide, these three; and the greatest of these is love.

*Whoever loves a brother or sister lives
in the light.*

Now by this we may be sure that we know
him, if we obey his commandments. Whoever
says, "I have come to know him," but does not
obey his commandments, is a liar, and in such a
person the truth does not exist; but whoever obeys
his word, truly in this person the love of God has
reached perfection. By this we may be sure that
we are in him: whoever says, "I abide in him,"
ought to walk just as he walked. Beloved, I am
writing you no new commandment, but an old
commandment that you have had from the beginning; the old commandment is the word that you
have heard. Yet I am writing you a new commandment that is true in him and in you, because the
darkness is passing away and the true light is already shining. Whoever says, "I am in the light,"
while hating a brother or sister, is still in the darkness. Whoever loves a brother or sister lives in
the light, and in such a person there is no cause
for stumbling. But whoever hates another believer
is in the darkness, walks in the darkness, and does
not know the way to go, because the darkness has
brought on blindness.

If we love one another God lives in us.

Beloved, since God loved us so much, we also ought to love one another. No one has ever seen God; if we love one another, God lives in us, and his love is perfected in us. By this we know that we abide in him and he in us, because he has given us of his Spirit. And we have seen and do testify that the Father has sent his Son as the Savior of the world. God abides in those who confess that Jesus is the Son of God, and they abide in God. So we have known and believe the love that God has for us. God is love, and those who abide in love abide in God, and God abides in them. Love has been perfected among us in this: that we may have boldness on the day of judgment, because as he is, so are we in this world. There is no fear in love, but perfect love casts out fear; for fear has to do with punishment, and whoever fears has not reached perfection in love.

James 3:1-10   **A-5**

No one can tame the tongue.

Not many of you should become teachers, my brothers and sisters, for you know that we who teach will be judged with greater strictness. For all of us make many mistakes. Anyone who makes no mistakes in speaking is perfect, able to keep the whole body in check with a bridle. If we put bits into the mouths of horses to make them obey us, we guide their whole bodies. Or look at ships: they are so large that it takes strong winds to drive them, yet they are guided by a very small rudder wherever the will of the pilot directs. So also the tongue is a small member, yet it boasts of great exploits. How great a forest is set ablaze by a small fire! And the tongue is a fire. The tongue is placed among our members as a world of iniquity; it stains the whole body, sets on fire the cycle of nature, and is itself set on fire by hell. For every species of beast and bird, of reptile and sea creature, can be tamed and has been tamed by the human species, but no one can tame the tongue— a restless evil, full of deadly poison. With it we bless the Lord and Father, and with it we curse those who are made in the likeness of God. From the same mouth come blessing and cursing. My brothers and sisters, this ought not to be so.

Psalm 32   A-6

Happy are those whose transgression is
    forgiven,
whose sin is covered.
Happy are those to whom the Lord imputes
    no iniquity,
and in whose spirit there is no deceit.

While I kept silence, my body wasted away
through my groaning all day long.
For day and night your hand was heavy upon
    me;

my strength was dried up as by the heat of
   summer.

Then I acknowledged my sin to you,
and I did not hide my iniquity;
I said, "I will confess my transgressions to the
   LORD,"
and you forgave the guilt of my sin.

Therefore let all who are faithful offer prayer
   to you;
at a time of distress, the rush of mighty waters
shall not reach them.
You are a hiding place for me;
you preserve me from trouble;
you surround me with glad cries of
   deliverance.
I will instruct you and teach you the way
   you should go;
I will counsel you with my eye upon you.
Do not be like a horse or a mule, without
   understanding,
whose temper must be curbed with bit
   and bridle,
else it will not stay near you.
Many are the torments of the wicked,
but steadfast love surrounds those who trust
   in the LORD.
Be glad in the LORD and rejoice, O righteous,
and shout for joy, all you upright in heart.

Have mercy on me, O God,
according to your steadfast love;
according to your abundant mercy
blot out my transgressions.
Wash me thoroughly from my iniquity,
and cleanse me from my sin.

For I know my transgressions,
and my sin is ever before me.
Against you, you alone, have I sinned,
and done what is evil in your sight,
so that you are justified in your sentence
and blameless when you pass judgment.
Indeed, I was born guilty,
a sinner when my mother conceived me.

You desire truth in the inward being;
therefore teach me wisdom in my secret heart.
Purge me with hyssop, and I shall be clean;
wash me, and I shall be whiter than snow.
Let me hear joy and gladness;
let the bones that you have crushed rejoice.
Hide your face from my sins,
and blot out all my iniquities.

Create in me a clean heart, O God,
and put a new and right spirit within me.
Do not cast me away from your presence,
and do not take your holy spirit from me.
Restore to me the joy of your salvation,
and sustain in me a willing spirit.

Then I will teach transgressors your ways,
and sinners will return to you.
Deliver me from bloodshed, O God,
O God of my salvation,
and my tongue will sing aloud of your
 deliverance.

O LORD, open my lips,
and my mouth will declare your praise.
For you have no delight in sacrifice;
if I were to give a burnt offering, you would
 not be pleased.
The sacrifice acceptable to God is a
 broken spirit;
a broken and contrite heart,
O God, you will not despise.

Do good to Zion in your good pleasure;
rebuild the walls of Jerusalem,
then you will delight in right sacrifices,
in burnt offerings and whole burnt offerings;
then bulls will be offered on your altar.

Psalm 103   A-8

Bless the LORD, O my soul,
and all that is within me,
bless his holy name.
Bless the LORD, O my soul,
and do not forget all his benefits –
who forgives all your iniquity,
who heals all your diseases,
who redeems your life from the Pit,

who crowns you with steadfast love and mercy,
who satisfies you with good as long as
    you live
so that your youth is renewed like the eagle's.

The LORD works vindication
and justice for all who are oppressed.
He made known his ways to Moses,
his acts to the people of Israel.
The LORD is merciful and gracious,
slow to anger and abounding in steadfast love.
He will not always accuse,
nor will he keep his anger forever.
He does not deal with us according to our sins,
nor repay us according to our iniquities.
For as the heavens are high above the earth,
so great is his steadfast love toward those who
    fear him;
as far as the east is from the west,
so far he removes our transgressions from us.
As a father has compassion for his children,
so the LORD has compassion for those
    who fear him.
For he knows how we were made;
he remembers that we are dust.

As for mortals, their days are like grass;
they flourish like a flower of the field;
for the wind passes over it, and it is gone,
and its place knows it no more.
But the steadfast love of the LORD is
    from everlasting to everlasting

on those who fear him,
and his righteousness to children's children,
to those who keep his covenant
and remember to do his commandments.

The LORD has established his throne in
    the heavens,
and his kingdom rules over all.
Bless the LORD, O you his angels,
you mighty ones who do his bidding,
obedient to his spoken word.
Bless the LORD, all his hosts,
his ministers that do his will.
Bless the LORD, all his works,
in all places of his dominion.
Bless the LORD, O my soul.

Psalm 145   A-9

I will extol you, my God and King,
and bless your name forever and ever.
Every day I will bless you,
and praise your name forever and ever.
Great is the LORD, and greatly to be praised;
his greatness is unsearchable.

One generation shall laud your works
    to another,
and shall declare your mighty acts.
On the glorious splendour of your majesty,
and on your wondrous works, I will meditate.
The might of your awesome deeds shall
    be proclaimed,

and I will declare your greatness.
They shall celebrate the fame of your
    abundant goodness,
and shall sing aloud of your righteousness.

The Lord is gracious and merciful,
slow to anger and abounding in steadfast love.
The Lord is good to all,
and his compassion is over all that he
    has made.

All your works shall give thanks to you,
    O Lord,
and all your faithful shall bless you.
They shall speak of the glory of your
    kingdom,
and tell of your power,
to make known to all people your
    mighty deeds,
and the glorious splendour of your kingdom.
Your kingdom is an everlasting kingdom,
and your dominion endures throughout all
    generations.
The Lord is faithful in all his words,
and gracious in all his deeds.
The Lord upholds all who are falling,
and raises up all who are bowed down.
The eyes of all look to you,
and you give them their food in due season.
You open your hand,
satisfying the desire of every living thing.
The Lord is just in all his ways,

and kind in all his doings.
The LORD is near to all who call on him,
to all who call on him in truth.
He fulfills the desire of all who fear him;
he also hears their cry, and saves them.
The LORD watches over all who love him,
but all the wicked he will destroy.

My mouth will speak the praise of the LORD,
and all flesh will bless his holy name forever
and ever.

Psalm 104 A-10

Bless the LORD, O my soul.
O LORD my God, you are very great.
You are clothed with honour and majesty,
wrapped in light as with a garment.
You stretch out the heavens like a tent,
you set the beams of your chambers on
the waters,
you make the clouds your chariot,
you ride on the wings of the wind,
you make the winds your messengers,
fire and flame your ministers.

You set the earth on its foundations,
so that it shall never be shaken.
You cover it with the deep as with a garment;
the waters stood above the mountains.
At your rebuke they flee;
at the sound of your thunder they take to flight.

They rose up to the mountains, ran down
    to the valleys
to the place that you appointed for them.
You set a boundary that they may not pass,
so that they might not again cover the earth.

You make springs gush forth in the valleys;
they flow between the hills,
giving drink to every wild animal;
the wild asses quench their thirst.
By the streams the birds of the air have
    their habitation;
they sing among the branches.
From your lofty abode you water the
    mountains;
the earth is satisfied with the fruit of your work.

You cause the grass to grow for the cattle,
and plants for people to use,
to bring forth food from the earth,
and wine to gladden the human heart,
oil to make the face shine,
and bread to strengthen the human heart.
The trees of the LORD are watered abundantly,
the cedars of Lebanon that he planted.
In them the birds build their nests;
the stork has its home in the fir trees.
The high mountains are for the wild goats;
the rocks are a refuge for the coneys.
You have made the moon to mark the seasons;
the sun knows its time for setting.

You make darkness, and it is night,
when all the animals of the forest come
    creeping out.
The young lions roar for their prey,
seeking their food from God.
When the sun rises, they withdraw
and lie down in their dens.
People go out to their work
and to their labour until the evening.

O LORD, how manifold are your works!
In wisdom you have made them all;
the earth is full of your creatures.
Yonder is the sea, great and wide,
creeping things innumerable are there,
living things both small and great.
There go the ships,
and Leviathan that you formed to sport in it.

These all look to you
to give them their food in due season;
when you give to them, they gather it up;
when you open your hand, they are filled with
    good things.
When you hide your face, they are dismayed;
when you take away their breath, they die
and return to their dust.
When you send forth your spirit, they are
    created;
and you renew the face of the ground.

May the glory of the Lord endure forever;
may the Lord rejoice in his works –
who looks on the earth and it trembles,
who touches the mountains and they smoke.
I will sing to the Lord as long as I live;
I will sing praise to my God while I have
    being.
May my meditation be pleasing to him,
for I rejoice in the Lord.
Let sinners be consumed from the earth,
and let the wicked be no more.
Bless the Lord, O my soul.
Praise the Lord!

Section B

For those who are discouraged by their weakness and sin

Isaiah 5:1-7   B-1
The vineyard of the LORD of hosts
is the house of Israel.

Ezekiel 36:23-28   B-2
A new heart I will give you, and a new
spirit I will put within you.

Matthew 4:12-17, 23-25   B-3
The kingdom of heaven has come near.

Matthew 5:1-12   B-4
Blessed are the poor in spirit.

Matthew 9:1-8   B-5
They glorified God, who had given such
authority to human beings.

Matthew 5:13-16   B-6
You are the light of the world.

Hebrews 12:1-4   B-7
Let us run with perseverance the race that is
set before us.

Romans 7:18-25a   B-8
Who will rescue me from this body of
death?

2 Peter 1:2-7   B-9
*Through these things, you may become
participants of the divine nature.*

Psalm 56   B-10
Psalm 65   B-11
Psalm 64   B-12

The vineyard of the LORD of hosts is
the house of Israel.

Let me sing for my beloved
my love-song concerning his vineyard:
My beloved had a vineyard on a very
    fertile hill.
He dug it and cleared it of stones,
and planted it with choice vines;
he built a watchtower in the midst of it,
and hewed out a wine vat in it;
he expected it to yield grapes,
but it yielded wild grapes.

And now, inhabitants of Jerusalem
and people of Judah,
judge between me
and my vineyard.
What more was there to do for my vineyard
that I have not done in it?
When I expected it to yield grapes,
why did it yield wild grapes?

And now I will tell you
what I will do to my vineyard.
I will remove its hedge,
and it shall be devoured;
I will break down its wall,
and it shall be trampled down.
I will make it a waste;
it shall not be pruned or hoed,

and it shall be overgrown with briers
    and thorns;
I will also command the clouds
that they rain no rain upon it.
For the vineyard of the LORD of hosts
is the house of Israel,
and the people of Judah are his pleasant
    planting;
he expected justice,
but saw bloodshed;
righteousness, but heard a cry!

Ezekiel 36:23-28   B-2

*A new heart I will give you, and a new spirit
I will put within you.*

I will sanctify my great name, which has been
profaned among the nations, and which you have
profaned among them; and the nations shall know
that I am the LORD, says the LORD God, when
through you I display my holiness before their
eyes. I will take you from the nations, and gather
you from all the countries, and bring you into your
own land. I will sprinkle clean water upon you,
and you shall be clean from all your
uncleannesses, and from all your idols I will
cleanse you. A new heart I will give you, and a
new spirit I will put within you; and I will remove from your body the heart of stone and give
you a heart of flesh. I will put my spirit within
you, and make you follow my statutes and be care-

ful to observe my ordinances. Then you shall live in the land that I gave to your ancestors; and you shall be my people, and I will be your God.

Matthew 4:12-17, 23-25 B-3
The kingdom of heaven has come near.

Now when Jesus heard that John had been arrested, he withdrew to Galilee. He left Nazareth and made his home in Capernaum by the sea, in the territory of Zebulun and Naphtali, so that what had been spoken through the prophet Isaiah might be fulfilled: "Land of Zebulun, land of Naphtali, on the road by the sea, across the Jordan, Galilee of the Gentiles – the people who sat in darkness have seen a great light, and for those who sat in the region and shadow of death light has dawned." From that time Jesus began to proclaim, "Repent, for the kingdom of heaven has come near." Jesus went throughout Galilee, teaching in their synagogues and proclaiming the good news of the kingdom and curing every disease and every sickness among the people. So his fame spread throughout all Syria, and they brought to him all the sick, those who were afflicted with various diseases and pains, demoniacs, epileptics, and paralytics, and he cured them. And great crowds followed him from Galilee, the Decapolis, Jerusalem, Judea, and from beyond the Jordan.

Blessed are the poor in spirit.

When Jesus saw the crowds, he went up the mountain; and after he sat down, his disciples came to him. Then he began to speak, and taught them, saying: "Blessed are the poor in spirit, for theirs is the kingdom of heaven. Blessed are those who mourn, for they will be comforted. Blessed are the meek, for they will inherit the earth. Blessed are those who hunger and thirst for righteousness, for they will be filled. Blessed are the merciful, for they will receive mercy. Blessed are the pure in heart, for they will see God. Blessed are the peacemakers, for they will be called children of God. Blessed are those who are persecuted for righteousness' sake, for theirs is the kingdom of heaven. Blessed are you when people revile you and persecute you and utter all kinds of evil against you falsely on my account. Rejoice and be glad, for your reward is great in heaven, for in the same way they persecuted the prophets who were before you."

Matthew 9:1-8 **B-5**

They glorified God, who had given such authority to human beings.

And after getting into a boat he crossed the sea and came to his own town. And just then some people were carrying a paralyzed man lying on a bed. When Jesus saw their faith, he said to the

paralytic, "Take heart, son; your sins are forgiven."
Then some of the scribes said to themselves, "This
man is blaspheming." But Jesus, perceiving their
thoughts, said, "Why do you think evil in your
hearts? For which is easier, to say, 'Your sins are
forgiven,' or to say, 'Stand up and walk'? But so
that you may know that the Son of Man has authority on earth to forgive sins" – he then said to
the paralytic – "Stand up, take your bed and go to
your home." And he stood up and went to his
home. When the crowds saw it, they were filled
with awe, and they glorified God, who had given
such authority to human beings.

Matthew 5:13-16   B-6
You are the light of the world.

Jesus said to his disciples: "You are the salt of
the earth; but if salt has lost its taste, how can its
saltiness be restored? It is no longer good for anything, but is thrown out and trampled under foot.
You are the light of the world. A city built on a
hill cannot be hid. No one after lighting a lamp
puts it under the bushel basket, but on the
lampstand, and it gives light to all in the house.
In the same way, let your light shine before others, so that they may see your good works and
give glory to your Father in heaven."

Hebrews 12:1-4

Let us run with perseverance the race that is set before us.

Therefore, since we are surrounded by so great a cloud of witnesses, let us also lay aside every weight and the sin that clings so closely, and let us run with perseverance the race that is set before us, looking to Jesus the pioneer and perfecter of our faith, who for the sake of the joy that was set before him endured the cross, disregarding its shame, and has taken his seat at the right hand of the throne of God. Consider him who endured such hostility against himself from sinners, so that you may not grow weary or lose heart. In your struggle against sin you have not yet resisted to the point of shedding your blood.

Romans 7:18-25a

Who will rescue me from this body of death?

For I know that nothing good dwells within me, that is, in my flesh. I can will what is right, but I cannot do it. For I do not do the good I want, but the evil I do not want is what I do. Now if I do what I do not want, it is no longer I that do it, but sin that dwells within me. So I find it to be a law that when I want to do what is good, evil lies close at hand. For I delight in the law of God in my inmost self, but I see in my members another law at war with the law of my mind, making me captive to the law of sin that dwells in my members.

Wretched man that I am! Who will rescue me from this body of death? Thanks be to God through Jesus Christ our Lord!

2 Peter 1:2-7 B-9

Through these things, you may become participants of the divine nature.

May grace and peace be yours in abundance in the knowledge of God and of Jesus our Lord. His divine power has given us everything needed for life and godliness, through the knowledge of him who called us by his own glory and goodness. Thus he has given us, through these things, his precious and very great promises, so that through them you may escape from the corruption that is in the world because of lust, and may become participants of the divine nature. For this very reason, you must make every effort to support your faith with goodness, and goodness with knowledge, and knowledge with self-control, and self-control with endurance, and endurance with godliness, and godliness with mutual affection, and mutual affection with love.

Psalm 56 B-10

Be gracious to me, O God, for people trample
  on me;
all day long foes oppress me;
my enemies trample on me all day long,
for many fight against me.

O Most High, when I am afraid,
I put my trust in you.
In God, whose word I praise,
in God I trust; I am not afraid;
what can flesh do to me?

All day long they seek to injure my cause;
all their thoughts are against me for evil.
They stir up strife, they lurk,
they watch my steps.
As they hoped to have my life,
so repay them for their crime;
in wrath cast down the peoples, O God!

You have kept count of my tossings;
put my tears in your bottle.
Are they not in your record?
Then my enemies will retreat in the day when
    I call.
This I know, that God is for me.
In God, whose word I praise,
in the LORD, whose word I praise,
in God I trust; I am not afraid.
What can a mere mortal do to me?

My vows to you I must perform, O God;
I will render thank offerings to you.
For you have delivered my soul from death,
and my feet from falling,
so that I may walk before God in the light
    of life.

Praise is due to you, O God, in Zion;
and to you shall vows be performed,
O you who answer prayer!
To you all flesh shall come.
When deeds of iniquity overwhelm us,
you forgive our transgressions.
Happy are those whom you choose and
    bring near
to live in your courts.
We shall be satisfied with the goodness of your
    house,
your holy temple.

By awesome deeds you answer us with
    deliverance,
O God of our salvation;
you are the hope of all the ends of the earth
and of the farthest seas.
By your strength you established the
    mountains;
you are girded with might.
You silence the roaring of the seas,
the roaring of their waves,
the tumult of the peoples.
Those who live at earth's farthest bounds are
    awed by your signs;
you make the gateways of the morning and
    the evening shout for joy.

You visit the earth and water it,
you greatly enrich it;

the river of God is full of water;
you provide the people with grain,
for so you have prepared it.
You water its furrows abundantly,
settling its ridges, softening it with showers,
and blessing its growth.
You crown the year with your bounty;
your wagon tracks overflow with richness.
The pastures of the wilderness overflow,
the hills gird themselves with joy,
the meadows clothe themselves with flocks,
the valleys deck themselves with grain,
they shout and sing together for joy.

Psalm 64 B-12

Hear my voice, O God, in my complaint;
preserve my life from the dread enemy.
Hide me from the secret plots of the wicked,
from the scheming of evildoers,
who whet their tongues like swords,
who aim bitter words like arrows,
shooting from ambush at the blameless;
they shoot suddenly and without fear.
They hold fast to their evil purpose;
they talk of laying snares secretly,
thinking, "Who can see us?
Who can search out our crimes?
We have thought out a cunningly conceived
plot."

For the human heart and mind are deep.

But God will shoot his arrow at them;
they will be wounded suddenly.
Because of their tongue he will bring them to
   ruin;
all who see them will shake with horror.
Then everyone will fear;
they will tell what God has brought about,
and ponder what he has done.

Let the righteous rejoice in the LORD
and take refuge in him.
Let all the upright in heart glory.

Section C

For those who need to pass from legalism to commandments as signs of love

Exodus 20:1-17   C-1
The law is a grateful response to what God has done for us.

Deuteronomy 6:4-13   C-2
*You shall love the L*ORD *your God with all your heart.*

Joel 2:12-18   C-3
Rend your hearts, and not your clothing.

John 15:1-8   C-4
Those who abide in me and I in them bear much fruit.

1 John 4:11-18   C-5
If we love one another God lives in us.

1 Corinthians 12:31–13:13   C-6
Faith, hope, and love abide, these three; and the greatest of these is love.

Psalm 105   C-7

Psalm 145   C-8

The law is a grateful response to what God has done for us.

Then God spoke all these words: I am the LORD your God, who brought you out of the land of Egypt, out of the house of slavery; you shall have no other gods before me. You shall not make for yourself an idol, whether in the form of anything that is in heaven above, or that is on the earth beneath, or that is in the water under the earth. You shall not bow down to them or worship them; for I the LORD your God am a jealous God, punishing children for the iniquity of parents, to the third and the fourth generation of those who reject me, but showing steadfast love to the thousandth generation of those who love me and keep my commandments. You shall not make wrongful use of the name of the LORD your God, for the LORD will not acquit anyone who misuses his name. Remember the sabbath day, and keep it holy. Six days you shall labour and do all your work. But the seventh day is a sabbath to the LORD your God; you shall not do any work – you, your son or your daughter, your male or female slave, your livestock, or the alien resident in your towns. For in six days the LORD made heaven and earth, the sea, and all that is in them, but rested the seventh day; therefore the LORD blessed the sabbath day and consecrated it. Honour your father and your mother, so that your days may be long in the land that the LORD your God is giving you. You shall not murder. You shall not commit adultery. You shall not steal. You shall not bear false witness against your neighbour. You shall not covet your neighbour's house; you shall not covet your neighbour's wife, or male or female slave, or ox, or donkey, or anything that belongs to your neighbour.

Deuteronomy 6:4-13 **C-2**

You shall love the LORD your God with all your heart.

Moses spoke to the people and said:

Hear, O Israel: The LORD is our God, the LORD alone. You shall love the LORD your God with all your heart, and with all your soul, and with all your might. Keep these words that I am commanding you today in your heart. Recite them to your children and talk about them when you are at home and when you are away, when you lie down and when you rise. Bind them as a sign on your hand, fix them as an emblem on your forehead, and write them on the doorposts of your house and on your gates. When the LORD your God has brought you into the land that he swore to your ancestors, to Abraham, to Isaac, and to Jacob, to give you – a land with fine, large cities that you did not build, houses filled with all sorts of goods that you did not fill, hewn cisterns that you did not hew, vineyards and olive groves that you did not plant – and when you have eaten your fill, take care that

you do not forget the LORD, who brought you out
of the land of Egypt, out of the house of slavery.
The LORD your God you shall fear; him you shall
serve, and by his name alone you shall swear.

Joel 2:12-18   C-3

Rend your hearts and not your clothing.

Yet even now, says the LORD,
return to me with all your heart,
with fasting, with weeping, and with
    mourning;
rend your hearts and not your clothing.
Return to the LORD, your God,
for he is gracious and merciful,
slow to anger, and abounding in steadfast love,
and relents from punishing.
Who knows whether he will not turn
    and relent,
and leave a blessing behind him,
a grain offering and a drink offering
for the LORD, your God?

Blow the trumpet in Zion; sanctify a fast;
call a solemn assembly; gather the people.
Sanctify the congregation; assemble the aged;
gather the children, even infants at the breast.
Let the bridegroom leave his room,
and the bride her canopy.

Between the vestibule and the altar
let the priests, the ministers of
    the LORD, weep.

Let them say, "Spare your people, O LORD,
and do not make your heritage a mockery,
a byword among the nations.
Why should it be said among the peoples,
'Where is their God?'"

Then the LORD became jealous for his land,
and had pity on his people.

John 15:1-8 C-4

Those who abide in me and I in them bear much fruit.

Jesus said to his disciples:

"I am the true vine, and my Father is the vinegrower. He removes every branch in me that bears no fruit. Every branch that bears fruit he prunes to make it bear more fruit. You have already been cleansed by the word that I have spoken to you. Abide in me as I abide in you. Just as the branch cannot bear fruit by itself unless it abides in the vine, neither can you unless you abide in me. I am the vine, you are the branches. Those who abide in me and I in them bear much fruit, because apart from me you can do nothing. Whoever does not abide in me is thrown away like a branch and withers; such branches are gathered, thrown into the fire, and burned. If you abide in me, and my words abide in you, ask for whatever you wish, and it will be done for you. My Father is glorified by this, that you bear much fruit and become my disciples."

If we love one another God lives in us.

Beloved, since God loved us so much, we also ought to love one another. No one has ever seen God; if we love one another, God lives in us, and his love is perfected in us. By this we know that we abide in him and he in us, because he has given us of his Spirit. And we have seen and do testify that the Father has sent his Son as the Saviour of the world. God abides in those who confess that Jesus is the Son of God, and they abide in God. So we have known and believe the love that God has for us. God is love, and those who abide in love abide in God, and God abides in them. Love has been perfected among us in this: that we may have boldness on the day of judgment, because as he is, so are we in this world. There is no fear in love, but perfect love casts out fear; for fear has to do with punishment, and whoever fears has not reached perfection in love.

1 Corinthians 12:31 – 13:13   **C-6**

Faith, hope, and love abide, these three; and the greatest of these is love.

But strive for the greater gifts. And I will show you a still more excellent way.

If I speak in the tongues of mortals and of angels, but do not have love, I am a noisy gong or a clanging cymbal. And if I have prophetic powers, and understand all mysteries and all knowledge, and if I have all faith, so as to remove mountains, but do not have love, I am nothing. If I give away all my possessions, and if I hand over my body so that I may boast, but do not have love, I gain nothing. Love is patient; love is kind; love is not envious or boastful or arrogant or rude. It does not insist on its own way; it is not irritable or resentful; it does not rejoice in wrongdoing, but rejoices in the truth. It bears all things, believes all things, hopes all things, endures all things. Love never ends. But as for prophecies, they will come to an end; as for tongues, they will cease; as for knowledge, it will come to an end. For we know only in part, and we prophesy only in part; but when the complete comes, the partial will come to an end. When I was a child, I spoke like a child, I thought like a child, I reasoned like a child; when I became an adult, I put an end to childish ways. For now we see in a mirror, dimly, but then we will see face to face. Now I know only in part; then I will know fully, even as I have been fully known. And now faith, hope, and love abide, these three; and the greatest of these is love.

Psalm 105   C-7

O give thanks to the LORD, call on his name,
make known his deeds among the peoples.
Sing to him, sing praises to him;
tell of all his wonderful works.
Glory in his holy name;

let the hearts of those who seek the LORD
    rejoice.
Seek the LORD and his strength;
seek his presence continually.
Remember the wonderful works he has done,
his miracles, and the judgments he uttered,
O offspring of his servant Abraham,
children of Jacob, his chosen ones.

He is the LORD our God;
his judgments are in all the earth.
He is mindful of his covenant forever,
of the word that he commanded, for
    a thousand generations,
the covenant that he made with Abraham,
his sworn promise to Isaac,
which he confirmed to Jacob as a statute,
to Israel as an everlasting covenant,
saying, "To you I will give the land of Canaan
as your portion for an inheritance."

When they were few in number,
of little account, and strangers in it,
wandering from nation to nation,
from one kingdom to another people,
he allowed no one to oppress them;
he rebuked kings on their account,
saying, "Do not touch my anointed ones;
do my prophets no harm."

When he summoned famine against the land,
and broke every staff of bread,
he had sent a man ahead of them,

Joseph, who was sold as a slave.
His feet were hurt with fetters,
his neck was put in a collar of iron;
until what he had said came to pass,
the word of the LORD kept testing him.
The king sent and released him;
the ruler of the peoples set him free.
He made him LORD of his house,
and ruler of all his possessions,
to instruct his officials at his pleasure,
and to teach his elders wisdom.

Then Israel came to Egypt;
Jacob lived as an alien in the land of Ham.
And the LORD made his people very fruitful,
made them stronger than their foes,
whose hearts he then turned to hate
    his people,
to deal craftily with his servants.

He sent his servant Moses,
and Aaron whom he had chosen.
They performed his signs among them,
and miracles in the land of Ham.
He sent darkness, and made the land dark;
they rebelled against his words.
He turned their waters into blood,
and caused their fish to die.
Their land swarmed with frogs,
even in the chambers of their kings.
He spoke, and there came swarms of flies,
and gnats throughout their country.
He gave them hail for rain,

and lightning that flashed through their land.
He struck their vines and fig trees,
and shattered the trees of their country.
He spoke, and the locusts came,
and young locusts without number;
they devoured all the vegetation in their land,
and ate up the fruit of their ground.
He struck down all the firstborn in their land,
the first issue of all their strength.

Then he brought Israel out with silver and gold,
and there was no one among their tribes
    who stumbled.
Egypt was glad when they departed,
for dread of them had fallen upon it.
He spread a cloud for a covering,
and fire to give light by night.
They asked, and he brought quails,
and gave them food from heaven in
    abundance.
He opened the rock, and water gushed out;
it flowed through the desert like a river.
For he remembered his holy promise,
and Abraham, his servant.
So he brought his people out with joy,
his chosen ones with singing.
He gave them the lands of the nations,
and they took possession of the wealth
    of the peoples,
that they might keep his statutes
and observe his laws.
Praise the LORD!

I will extol you, my God and King,
and bless your name forever and ever.
Every day I will bless you,
and praise your name forever and ever.
Great is the LORD, and greatly to be praised;
his greatness is unsearchable.

One generation shall laud your works to
     another,
and shall declare your mighty acts.
On the glorious splendour of your majesty,
and on your wondrous works, I will meditate.
The might of your awesome deeds shall
     be proclaimed,
and I will declare your greatness.
They shall celebrate the fame of your
     abundant goodness,
and shall sing aloud of your righteousness.

The LORD is gracious and merciful,
slow to anger and abounding in steadfast love.
The LORD is good to all,
and his compassion is over all that he
     has made.

All your works shall give thanks to you,
     O LORD,
and all your faithful shall bless you.
They shall speak of the glory of your
     kingdom,
and tell of your power,

to make known to all people your
    mighty deeds,
and the glorious splendour of your kingdom.
Your kingdom is an everlasting kingdom,
and your dominion endures throughout all
    generations.
The Lord is faithful in all his words,
and gracious in all his deeds.

The Lord upholds all who are falling,
and raises up all who are bowed down.
The eyes of all look to you,
and you give them their food in due season.
You open your hand,
satisfying the desire of every living thing.
The Lord is just in all his ways,
and kind in all his doings.
The Lord is near to all who call on him,
to all who call on him in truth.
He fulfills the desire of all who fear him;
he also hears their cry, and saves them.
The Lord watches over all who love him,
but all the wicked he will destroy.

My mouth will speak the praise of the Lord,
and all flesh will bless his holy name forever
    and ever.

Section D

For those who have recently returned after a long absence

Ezekiel 36:23-28   D-1
A new heart I will give you, and a new spirit I will put within you.

Ezekiel 18:21-28   D-2
If the wicked turn away from all their sins, they shall surely live.

Luke 15:1-10   D-3
There is joy in the presence of the angels of God over one sinner who repents.

Luke 15:1-3, 11-32   D-4
This brother of yours was dead and has come to life.

Ephesians 2:1-10   D-5
God raised us up with Christ and seated us with him in the heavenly places.

John 20:19-23   D-6
As the Father has sent me, so I send you: Receive the Holy Spirit.

Romans 6:19-23   D-7
You have been freed from sin and enslaved to God.

A new heart I will give you, and a new spirit I will put within you.

The LORD says this: I will sanctify my great name, which has been profaned among the nations, and which you have profaned among them; and the nations shall know that I am the LORD, says the LORD God, when through you I display my holiness before their eyes. I will take you from the nations, and gather you from all the countries, and bring you into your own land. I will sprinkle clean water upon you, and you shall be clean from all your uncleannesses, and from all your idols I will cleanse you. A new heart I will give you, and a new spirit I will put within you; and I will remove from your body the heart of stone and give you a heart of flesh. I will put my spirit within you, and make you follow my statutes and be careful to observe my ordinances. Then you shall live in the land that I gave to your ancestors; and you shall be my people, and I will be your God.

If the wicked turn away from all their sins, they shall surely live.

Thus says the LORD:

But if the wicked turn away from all their sins that they have committed and keep all my statutes and do what is lawful and right, they shall surely live; they shall not die. None of the transgressions that they have committed shall be re-membered against them; for the righteousness that they have done they shall live. Have I any pleasure in the death of the wicked, says the LORD God, and not rather that they should turn from their ways and live? But when the righteous turn away from their righteousness and commit iniquity and do the same abominable things that the wicked do, shall they live? None of the righteous deeds that they have done shall be remembered; for the treachery of which they are guilty and the sin they have committed, they shall die. Yet you say, "The way of the LORD is unfair." Hear now, O house of Israel: Is my way unfair? Is it not your ways that are unfair? When the righteous turn away from their righteousness and commit iniquity, they shall die for it; for the iniquity that they have committed they shall die. Again, when the wicked turn away from the wickedness they have committed and do what is lawful and right, they shall save their life. Because they considered and turned away from all the transgressions that they had committed, they shall surely live; they shall not die.

Luke 15:1-10   D-3

There is joy in the presence of the angels of God over one sinner who repents.

Now all the tax collectors and sinners were coming near to listen to him. And the Pharisees and the scribes were grumbling and saying, "This fellow welcomes sinners and eats with them." So he told them this parable: "Which one of you, having a hundred sheep and losing one of them, does not leave the ninety-nine in the wilderness and go after the one that is lost until he finds it? When he has found it, he lays it on his shoulders and rejoices. And when he comes home, he calls together his friends and neighbours, saying to them, 'Rejoice with me, for I have found my sheep that was lost.' Just so, I tell you, there will be more joy in heaven over one sinner who repents than over ninety-nine righteous persons who need no repentance. Or what woman having ten silver coins, if she loses one of them, does not light a lamp, sweep the house, and search carefully until she finds it? When she has found it, she calls together her friends and neighbours, saying, 'Rejoice with me, for I have found the coin that I had lost.' Just so, I tell you, there is joy in the presence of the angels of God over one sinner who repents."

Luke 15:1-3, 11-32   D-4

This brother of yours was dead and has come to life.

Now all the tax collectors and sinners were coming near to listen to him. And the Pharisees and the scribes were grumbling and saying, "This fellow welcomes sinners and eats with them." So he told them this parable:

"There was a man who had two sons. The younger of them said to his father, 'Father, give me the share of the property that will belong to me.' So he divided his property between them. A few days later the younger son gathered all he had and travelled to a distant country, and there he squandered his property in dissolute living. When he had spent everything, a severe famine took place throughout that country, and he began to be in need. So he went and hired himself out to one of the citizens of that country, who sent him to his fields to feed the pigs. He would gladly have filled himself with the pods that the pigs were eating; and no one gave him anything. But when he came to himself he said, 'How many of my father's hired hands have bread enough and to spare, but here I am dying of hunger! I will get up and go to my father, and I will say to him, "Father, I have sinned against heaven and before you; I am no longer worthy to be called your son; treat me like one of your hired hands."' "So he set off and went to his father. But while he was still far off, his father saw him and was filled with compassion; he ran and put his arms around him and kissed him. Then the son said to him, 'Father, I have sinned against heaven and before you; I am no longer worthy to be called your son.' But the father said to his slaves, 'Quickly, bring out a robe – the best one – and put it on him; put a ring on his finger and sandals on his feet. And get the fatted calf and kill it, and let us eat and celebrate; for this son of mine was dead and is alive again; he was lost and is found!' And they began to celebrate. Now his elder son was in the field; and when he came and approached the house, he heard music and dancing. He called one of the slaves and asked what was going on. He replied, 'Your brother has come, and your father has killed the fatted calf, because he has got him back safe and sound.' Then he became angry and refused to go in. His father came out and began to plead with him. But he answered his father, 'Listen! For all these years I have been working like a slave for you, and I have never disobeyed your command; yet you have never given me even a young goat so that I might celebrate with my friends. But when this son of yours came back, who has devoured your property with prostitutes, you killed the fatted calf for him!' Then the father said to him, 'Son, you are always with me, and all that is mine is yours. But we had to celebrate and rejoice, because this brother of yours was dead and has come to life; he was lost and has been found.' "

Ephesians 2:1-10   D-5

God raised us up with Christ and seated us with him in the heavenly places.

You were dead through the trespasses and sins in which you once lived, following the course of this world, following the ruler of the power of the air, the spirit that is now at work among those who are disobedient. All of us once lived among them in the passions of our flesh, following the desires of flesh and senses, and we were by nature children of wrath, like everyone else. But God, who is rich in mercy, out of the great love with which he loved us even when we were dead through our trespasses, made us alive together with Christ – by grace you have been saved – and raised us up with him and seated us with him in the heavenly places in Christ Jesus, so that in the ages to come he might show the immeasurable riches of his grace in kindness toward us in Christ Jesus. For by grace you have been saved through faith, and this is not your own doing; it is the gift of God – not the result of works, so that no one may boast. For we are what he has made us, created in Christ Jesus for good works, which God prepared beforehand to be our way of life.

John 20:19-23   **D-6**

As the Father has sent me, so I send you:
Receive the Holy Spirit.

When it was evening on that day, the first day of the week, and the doors of the house where the disciples had met were locked for fear of the Jews, Jesus came and stood among them and said, "Peace be with you." After he said this, he showed them his hands and his side. Then the disciples rejoiced when they saw the Lord. Jesus said to them again, "Peace be with you. As the Father has sent me, so I send you." When he had said this, he breathed on them and said to them, "Receive the Holy Spirit. If you forgive the sins of any, they are forgiven them; if you retain the sins of any, they are retained."

Romans 6:19-23   D-7

You have been freed from sin and enslaved to God.

I am speaking in human terms because of your natural limitations. For just as you once presented your members as slaves to impurity and to greater and greater iniquity, so now present your members as slaves to righteousness for sanctification. When you were slaves of sin, you were free in regard to righteousness. So what advantage did you then get from the things of which you now are ashamed? The end of those things is death. But now that you have been freed from sin and enslaved to God, the advantage you get is sanctification. The end is eternal life. For the wages of sin is death, but the free gift of God is eternal life in Christ Jesus our Lord.

Section E

For those who need to be reminded of God's great mercy and Fatherly love

Isaiah 55:1-11   E-1
  *Come to me so that you may live. I will
  make with you an everlasting covenant.*

Exodus 17:1-7   E-2
  *He showed him water, that the people
  might drink.*

Matthew 9:9-13   E-3
  *I have come to call not the righteous but
  sinners.*

Luke 19:1-10   E-4
  *The Son of Man came to seek out and to save
  the lost.*

Luke 23:33, 39-43   E-5
  *Jesus, remember me when you come into
  your kingdom.*

John 19:31-37   E-6
  *One of the soldiers pierced his side with a
  spear, and at once blood and water came out.*

Romans 3:21-25a, 28   E-7
   A person is justified by faith, not by law.

Ephesians 2:1-10   E-8
   God raised us up with Christ and seated
   us with him in the heavenly places.

Romans 5:6-11   E-9
   We were reconciled to God through
   the death of his Son; we will be saved
   by his life.
Psalm 105   E-10

*Come to me so that you may live. I will make
with you an everlasting covenant.*

Ho, everyone who thirsts, come to the waters;
and you that have no money, come, buy
and eat!
Come, buy wine and milk without money and
without price.
Why do you spend your money for that which
is not bread,
and your labour for that which does not satisfy?
Listen carefully to me, and eat what is good,
and delight yourselves in rich food.
Incline your ear, and come to me;
listen, so that you may live.
I will make with you an everlasting covenant,
my steadfast, sure love for David.
See, I made him a witness to the peoples,
a leader and commander for the peoples.
See, you shall call nations that you do
not know,
and nations that do not know you shall run
to you,
because of the LORD your God, the Holy One
of Israel,
for he has glorified you.

Seek the LORD while he may be found,
call upon him while he is near;
let the wicked forsake their way,
and the unrighteous their thoughts;

let them return to the LORD, that he may have
mercy on them,
 and to our God, for he will abundantly
pardon.
For my thoughts are not your thoughts,
nor are your ways my ways, says the LORD.
For as the heavens are higher than the earth,
so are my ways higher than your ways
and my thoughts than your thoughts.

For as the rain and the snow come down from
heaven,
and do not return there until they have
watered the earth,
making it bring forth and sprout,
giving seed to the sower and bread to the eater,
so shall my word be that goes out from
my mouth;
it shall not return to me empty,
but it shall accomplish that which I purpose,
and succeed in the thing for which I sent it.

Exodus 17:1-7   E-2

*He showed him water, that the people
might drink.*

From the wilderness of Sin the whole congregation of the Israelites journeyed by stages, as the
LORD commanded. They camped at Rephidim, but
there was no water for the people to drink. The
people quarrelled with Moses, and said, "Give us
water to drink." Moses said to them, "Why do

you quarrel with me? Why do you test the LORD?" But the people thirsted there for water; and the people complained against Moses and said, "Why did you bring us out of Egypt, to kill us and our children and livestock with thirst?" So Moses cried out to the LORD, "What shall I do with this people? They are almost ready to stone me." The LORD said to Moses, "Go on ahead of the people, and take some of the elders of Israel with you; take in your hand the staff with which you struck the Nile, and go. I will be standing there in front of you on the rock at Horeb. Strike the rock, and water will come out of it, so that the people may drink." Moses did so, in the sight of the elders of Israel. He called the place Massah and Meribah, because the Israelites quarrelled and tested the LORD, saying, "Is the LORD among us or not?"

Matthew 9:9-13 E-3

I have come to call not the righteous but sinners.

As Jesus was walking along, he saw a man called Matthew sitting at the tax booth; and he said to him, "Follow me." And he got up and followed him. And as he sat at dinner in the house, many tax collectors and sinners came and were sitting with him and his disciples. When the Pharisees saw this, they said to his disciples, "Why does your teacher eat with tax collectors and sinners?" But when he heard this, he said, "Those who are well have no need of a physician, but those who are sick. Go and learn what this means, 'I desire mercy, not sacrifice.' For I have come to call not the righteous but sinners."

Luke 19:1-10 E-4
The Son of Man came to seek out and to save the lost.

He entered Jericho and was passing through it. A man was there named Zacchaeus; he was a chief tax collector and was rich. He was trying to see who Jesus was, but on account of the crowd he could not, because he was short in stature. So he ran ahead and climbed a sycamore tree to see him, because he was going to pass that way. When Jesus came to the place, he looked up and said to him, "Zacchaeus, hurry and come down; for I must stay at your house today." So he hurried down and was happy to welcome him. All who saw it began to grumble and said, "He has gone to be the guest of one who is a sinner." Zacchaeus stood there and said to the Lord, "Look, half of my possessions, Lord, I will give to the poor; and if I have defrauded anyone of anything, I will pay back four times as much." Then Jesus said to him, "Today salvation has come to this house, because he too is a son of Abraham. For the Son of Man came to seek out and to save the lost."

*Jesus, remember me when you
come into your kingdom.*

When they came to the place that is called
The Skull, they crucified Jesus there with the
criminals, one on his right and one on his left.
One of the criminals who were hanged there kept
deriding him and saying, "Are you not the Mes-
siah? Save yourself and us!" But the other rebuked him, saying, "Do you not fear God, since
you are under the same sentence of condemna-
tion? And we indeed have been condemned
justly, for we are getting what we deserve for
our deeds, but this man has done nothing wrong."
Then he said, "Jesus, remember me when you
come into your kingdom." He replied, "Truly I
tell you, today you will be with me in Paradise."

John 19:31-37 E-6

*One of the soldiers pierced his side with a
spear, and at once blood and water came out.*

Since it was the day of Preparation, the Jews
did not want the bodies left on the cross during
the sabbath, especially because that sabbath was
a day of great solemnity. So they asked Pilate to
have the legs of the crucified men broken and the
bodies removed. Then the soldiers came and broke
the legs of the first and of the other who had been
crucified with him. But when they came to Jesus
and saw that he was already dead, they did not

break his legs. Instead, one of the soldiers pierced his side with a spear, and at once blood and water came out. (He who saw this has testified so that you also may believe. His testimony is true, and he knows that he tells the truth.) These things occurred so that the scripture might be fulfilled, "None of his bones shall be broken." And again another passage of scripture says, "They will look on the one whom they have pierced."

Romans 3:21-25a, 28   E-7

A person is justified by faith, not by law.

But now, apart from law, the righteousness of God has been disclosed, and is attested by the law and the prophets, the righteousness of God through faith in Jesus Christ for all who believe. For there is no distinction, since all have sinned and fall short of the glory of God; they are now justified by his grace as a gift, through the redemption that is in Christ Jesus, whom God put forward as a sacrifice of atonement by his blood, effective through faith. For we hold that a person is justified by faith apart from works prescribed by the law.

Ephesians 2:1-10   E-8

God raised us up with Christ and seated us with him in the heavenly places.

You were dead through the trespasses and sins in which you once lived, following the course of this world, following the ruler of the power of the air, the spirit that is now at work among those who are disobedient. All of us once lived among them in the passions of our flesh, following the desires of flesh and senses, and we were by nature children of wrath, like everyone else. But God, who is rich in mercy, out of the great love with which he loved us even when we were dead through our trespasses, made us alive together with Christ – by grace you have been saved – and raised us up with him and seated us with him in the heavenly places in Christ Jesus, so that in the ages to come he might show the immeasurable riches of his grace in kindness toward us in Christ Jesus. For by grace you have been saved through faith, and this is not your own doing; it is the gift of God – not the result of works, so that no one may boast. For we are what he has made us, created in Christ Jesus for good works, which God prepared beforehand to be our way of life.

Romans 5:6-11   E-9

We were reconciled to God through the death of his Son; we will be saved by his life.

For while we were still weak, at the right time Christ died for the ungodly. Indeed, rarely will anyone die for a righteous person – though perhaps for a good person someone might actually dare to die. But God proves his love for us in that while we still were sinners Christ died for us. Much more surely then, now that we have been justified by his blood, will we be saved through him from the wrath of God. For if while we were enemies, we were reconciled to God through the death of his Son, much more surely, having been reconciled, will we be saved by his life. But more than that, we even boast in God through our Lord Jesus Christ, through whom we have now received reconciliation.

Psalm 105 E-10

O give thanks to the Lord, call on his name,
make known his deeds among the peoples.
Sing to him, sing praises to him;
tell of all his wonderful works.
Glory in his holy name;
let the hearts of those who seek
    the Lord rejoice.
Seek the Lord and his strength;
seek his presence continually.
Remember the wonderful works he has done,
his miracles, and the judgments he uttered,
O offspring of his servant Abraham,
children of Jacob, his chosen ones.

He is the Lord our God;
his judgments are in all the earth.
He is mindful of his covenant forever,
of the word that he commanded, for a
    thousand generations,
the covenant that he made with Abraham,
his sworn promise to Isaac,

which he confirmed to Jacob as a statute,
to Israel as an everlasting covenant,
saying, "To you I will give the land of Canaan
as your portion for an inheritance."

When they were few in number,
of little account, and strangers in it,
wandering from nation to nation,
from one kingdom to another people,
he allowed no one to oppress them;
he rebuked kings on their account,
saying, "Do not touch my anointed ones;
do my prophets no harm."

When he summoned famine against the land,
and broke every staff of bread,
he had sent a man ahead of them,
Joseph, who was sold as a slave.
His feet were hurt with fetters,
his neck was put in a collar of iron;
until what he had said came to pass,
the word of the LORD kept testing him.
The king sent and released him;
the ruler of the peoples set him free.
He made him LORD of his house,
and ruler of all his possessions,
to instruct his officials at his pleasure,
and to teach his elders wisdom.

Then Israel came to Egypt;
Jacob lived as an alien in the land of Ham.
And the LORD made his people very fruitful,
made them stronger than their foes,

whose hearts he then turned to hate
   his people,
to deal craftily with his servants.

He sent his servant Moses,
and Aaron whom he had chosen.
They performed his signs among them,
and miracles in the land of Ham.
He sent darkness, and made the land dark;
they rebelled against his words.
He turned their waters into blood,
and caused their fish to die.
Their land swarmed with frogs,
even in the chambers of their kings.
He spoke, and there came swarms of flies,
and gnats throughout their country.
He gave them hail for rain,
and lightning that flashed through their land.
He struck their vines and fig trees,
and shattered the trees of their country.
He spoke, and the locusts came,
and young locusts without number;
they devoured all the vegetation in their land,
and ate up the fruit of their ground.
He struck down all the firstborn in their land,
the first issue of all their strength.

Then he brought Israel out with silver and gold,
and there was no one among their tribes
   who stumbled.
Egypt was glad when they departed,
for dread of them had fallen upon it.

He spread a cloud for a covering,
and fire to give light by night.
They asked, and he brought quails,
and gave them food from heaven in
    abundance.
He opened the rock, and water gushed out;
it flowed through the desert like a river.
For he remembered his holy promise,
and Abraham, his servant.
So he brought his people out with joy,
his chosen ones with singing.
He gave them the lands of the nations,
and they took possession of the wealth
    of the peoples,
that they might keep his statutes
and observe his laws. Praise the LORD!

Section F

For those who see that their lives must change

Jeremiah 2:1-3, 7-8, 12-13   F-1
They have forsaken me, the fountain
of living water, and dug out cisterns
for themselves.

Luke 13:1-9   F-2
Unless you repent, you will all perish
as they did.

Luke 18:9-14   F-3
The publican went down to his home justi-
fied;
the Pharisee did not.

Romans 13:4-14   F-4
The time has come, our salvation is near.

Galatians 5:18-25   F-5
Those who belong to Christ Jesus have
crucified the flesh with its passions.

Ephesians 6:10-20   F-6
Take up the whole armour of God so that
you may be able to stand firm.

James 1:19-27   F-7
Be not hearers who forget but doers who act.

James 2:14-24, 26   F-8
*For just as the body without the spirit is
dead, so faith without works is also dead.*

Psalm 32   F-9
Psalm 51   F-10
Psalm 102   F-11
Psalm 130   F-12
Psalm 23   F-13

They have forsaken me, the fountain
of living water, and dug out cisterns
for themselves.

The word of the LORD came to me, saying: Go
and proclaim in the hearing of Jerusalem, Thus
says the LORD:

I remember the devotion of your youth,
your love as a bride,
how you followed me in the wilderness,
in a land not sown.
Israel was holy to the LORD,
the first fruits of his harvest.
All who ate of it were held guilty;
disaster came upon them, says the LORD.

I brought you into a plentiful land
to eat its fruits and its good things.
But when you entered you defiled my land,
and made my heritage an abomination.
The priests did not say, "Where is the LORD?"
Those who handle the law did not know me;
the rulers transgressed against me;
the prophets prophesied by Baal,
and went after things that do not profit.

Be appalled, O heavens, at this,
be shocked, be utterly desolate,
    says the LORD,
for my people have committed two evils:
they have forsaken me,

the fountain of living water,
and dug out cisterns for themselves,
cracked cisterns that can hold no water.

Luke 13:1-9 F-2

*Unless you repent, you will all perish
as they did.*

At that very time there were some present who told him about the Galileans whose blood Pilate had mingled with their sacrifices. He asked them, "Do you think that because these Galileans suffered in this way they were worse sinners than all other Galileans? No, I tell you; but unless you repent, you will all perish as they did. Or those eighteen who were killed when the tower of Siloam fell on them – do you think that they were worse offenders than all the others living in Jerusalem? No, I tell you; but unless you repent, you will all perish just as they did." Then he told this parable: "A man had a fig tree planted in his vineyard; and he came looking for fruit on it and found none. So he said to the gardener, 'See here! For three years I have come looking for fruit on this fig tree, and still I find none. Cut it down! Why should it be wasting the soil?' He replied, 'Sir, let it alone for one more year, until I dig around it and put manure on it. If it bears fruit next year, well and good; but if not, you can cut it down.'"

The publican went down to his home justified;
the Pharisee did not.

He also told this parable to some who trusted in themselves that they were righteous and regarded others with contempt: "Two men went up to the temple to pray, one a Pharisee and the other a tax collector. The Pharisee, standing by himself, was praying thus, 'God, I thank you that I am not like other people: thieves, rogues, adulterers, or even like this tax collector. I fast twice a week; I give a tenth of all my income.' But the tax collector, standing far off, would not even look up to heaven, but was beating his breast and saying, 'God, be merciful to me, a sinner!' I tell you, this man went down to his home justified rather than the other; for all who exalt themselves will be humbled, but all who humble themselves will be exalted."

Romans 13:4-14   **F-4**

The time has come, our salvation is near.

But if you do what is wrong, you should be afraid, for the authority does not bear the sword in vain! It is the servant of God to execute wrath on the wrongdoer. Therefore one must be subject, not only because of wrath but also because of conscience. For the same reason you also pay taxes, for the authorities are God's servants, busy with this very thing. Pay to all what is due them – taxes to whom taxes are due, revenue to whom revenue is due, respect to whom respect is due, honour to whom honour is due.

Owe no one anything, except to love one another; for the one who loves another has fulfilled the law. The commandments, "You shall not commit adultery; You shall not murder; You shall not steal; You shall not covet"; and any other commandment, are summed up in this word, "Love your neighbour as yourself." Love does no wrong to a neighbour; therefore, love is the fulfilling of the law.

Besides this, you know what time it is, how it is now the moment for you to wake from sleep. For salvation is nearer to us now than when we became believers; the night is far gone, the day is near. Let us then lay aside the works of darkness and put on the armour of light; let us live honorably as in the day, not in revelling and drunkenness, not in debauchery and licentiousness, not in quarrelling and jealousy. Instead, put on the LORD Jesus Christ, and make no provision for the flesh, to gratify its desires.

Galatians 5:18-25 F-5

Those who belong to Christ Jesus have crucified the flesh with its passions.

But if you are led by the Spirit, you are not subject to the law. Now the works of the flesh are obvious: fornication, impurity, licentiousness, idolatry, sorcery, enmities, strife, jealousy, anger, quarrels, dissensions, factions, envy, drunkenness, carousing, and things like these. I am warning you, as I warned you before: those who do such things will not inherit the kingdom of God. By contrast, the fruit of the Spirit is love, joy, peace, patience, kindness, generosity, faithfulness, gentleness, and self-control. There is no law against such things. And those who belong to Christ Jesus have crucified the flesh with its passions and desires. If we live by the Spirit, let us also be guided by the Spirit. Let us not become conceited, competing against one another, envying one another.

Ephesians 6:10-20 F-6

Take up the whole armour of God so that you may be able to stand firm.

Finally, be strong in the Lord and in the strength of his power. Put on the whole armour of God, so that you may be able to stand against the wiles of the devil. For our struggle is not against enemies of blood and flesh, but against the rulers, against the authorities, against the cosmic powers of this present darkness, against the spiritual forces of evil in the heavenly places. Therefore take up the whole armour of God, so that you may be able to withstand on that evil day, and having done everything, to stand firm. Stand therefore, and fasten the belt of truth around your waist, and put on the breastplate of righteousness. As shoes for your feet put on whatever will make you ready to proclaim the gospel of peace. With all of these, take the shield of faith, with which you will be able to quench all the flaming arrows of the evil one. Take the helmet of salvation, and the sword of the Spirit, which is the word of God. Pray in the Spirit at all times in every prayer and supplication. To that end keep alert and always persevere in supplication for all the saints. Pray also for me, so that when I speak, a message may be given to me to make known with boldness the mystery of the gospel, for which I am an ambassador in chains. Pray that I may declare it boldly, as I must speak.

James 1:19-27 F-7

Be not hearers who forget but doers who act.

You must understand this, my beloved: let everyone be quick to listen, slow to speak, slow to anger; for your anger does not produce God's righteousness. Therefore rid yourselves of all sordidness and rank growth of wickedness, and welcome with meekness the implanted word that has the power to save your souls. But be doers of the word, and not merely hearers who deceive themselves. For if any are hearers of the word and not doers, they are like those who look at themselves in a mirror; for they look at themselves and, on going away, immediately forget what they were like. But those who look into the perfect law, the law of liberty, and persevere, being not hearers who forget but doers who act – they will be blessed in their doing. If any think they are religious, and do not bridle their tongues but deceive their hearts, their religion is worthless.

James 2:14-24, 26

For just as the body without the spirit is dead, so faith without works is also dead.

What good is it, my brothers and sisters, if you say you have faith but do not have works? Can faith save you? If a brother or sister is naked and lacks daily food, and one of you says to them, "Go in peace; keep warm and eat your fill," and yet you do not supply their bodily needs, what is the good of that? So faith by itself, if it has no works, is dead. But someone will say, "You have faith and I have works." Show me your faith apart from your works, and I by my works will show you my faith. You believe that God is one; you do well. Even the demons believe – and shudder. Do you want to be shown, you senseless person, that faith apart from works is barren? Was not our ancestor Abraham justified by works when he offered his son Isaac on the altar? You see that faith was active along with his works, and faith was brought to completion by the works. Thus the scripture was fulfilled that says, "Abraham believed God, and it was reckoned to him as right-eousness," and he was called the friend of God. You see that a person is justified by works and not by faith alone.

For just as the body without the spirit is dead, so faith without works is also dead.

Happy are those whose transgression
    is forgiven,
whose sin is covered.
Happy are those to whom the LORD
    imputes no iniquity,
and in whose spirit there is no deceit.

While I kept silence, my body wasted away
through my groaning all day long.
For day and night your hand was heavy
    upon me;
my strength was dried up as by the heat
    of summer.
Then I acknowledged my sin to you,
and I did not hide my iniquity;
I said, "I will confess my transgressions
    to the LORD,"
and you forgave the guilt of my sin.

Therefore let all who are faithful offer
    prayer to you;
at a time of distress, the rush of mighty waters
shall not reach them.
You are a hiding place for me;
you preserve me from trouble;
you surround me with glad cries of
    deliverance.

I will instruct you and teach you the way you
    should go;

I will counsel you with my eye upon you.
Do not be like a horse or a mule, without
    understanding,
whose temper must be curbed with bit
    and bridle,
else it will not stay near you.

Many are the torments of the wicked,
but steadfast love surrounds those who
    trust in the LORD.
Be glad in the LORD and rejoice, O righteous,
and shout for joy, all you upright in heart.

Psalm 51   F-10

Have mercy on me, O God,
according to your steadfast love;
according to your abundant mercy
blot out my transgressions.
Wash me thoroughly from my iniquity,
and cleanse me from my sin.

For I know my transgressions,
and my sin is ever before me.
Against you, you alone, have I sinned,
and done what is evil in your sight,
so that you are justified in your sentence
and blameless when you pass judgment.
Indeed, I was born guilty,
a sinner when my mother conceived me.

You desire truth in the inward being;
therefore teach me wisdom in my secret heart.
Purge me with hyssop, and I shall be clean;

wash me, and I shall be whiter than snow.
Let me hear joy and gladness;
let the bones that you have crushed rejoice.
Hide your face from my sins,
and blot out all my iniquities.

Create in me a clean heart, O God,
and put a new and right spirit within me.
Do not cast me away from your presence,
and do not take your holy spirit from me.
Restore to me the joy of your salvation,
and sustain in me a willing spirit.

Then I will teach transgressors your ways,
and sinners will return to you.
Deliver me from bloodshed, O God,
O God of my salvation,
and my tongue will sing aloud of
    your deliverance.

O LORD, open my lips,
and my mouth will declare your praise.
For you have no delight in sacrifice;
if I were to give a burnt offering, you
    would not be pleased.
The sacrifice acceptable to God is a
    broken spirit;
a broken and contrite heart,
O God, you will not despise.

Do good to Zion in your good pleasure;
rebuild the walls of Jerusalem,
then you will delight in right sacrifices,
in burnt offerings and whole burnt offerings;
then bulls will be offered on your altar.

Hear my prayer, O LORD;
let my cry come to you.
Do not hide your face from me in the day
    of my distress.
Incline your ear to me;
answer me speedily in the day when I call.
For my days pass away like smoke,
and my bones burn like a furnace.
My heart is stricken and withered like grass;
I am too wasted to eat my bread.
Because of my loud groaning
my bones cling to my skin.
I am like an owl of the wilderness,
like a little owl of the waste places.
I lie awake;
I am like a lonely bird on the housetop.
All day long my enemies taunt me;
those who deride me use my name for a curse.
For I eat ashes like bread,
and mingle tears with my drink,
because of your indignation and anger;
for you have lifted me up and thrown me aside.
My days are like an evening shadow;
I wither away like grass.
But you, O LORD, are enthroned forever;
your name endures to all generations.
You will rise up and have compassion on Zion,
for it is time to favour it;

the appointed time has come.
For your servants hold its stones dear,
and have pity on its dust.
The nations will fear the name of the LORD,
and all the kings of the earth your glory.
For the LORD will build up Zion;
he will appear in his glory.
He will regard the prayer of the destitute,
and will not despise their prayer.

Let this be recorded for a generation to come,
so that a people yet unborn may praise
    the LORD:
that he looked down from his holy height,
from heaven the LORD looked at the earth,
to hear the groans of the prisoners,
to set free those who were doomed to die;
so that the name of the LORD
may be declared in Zion,
and his praise in Jerusalem,
when peoples gather together,
and kingdoms, to worship the LORD.

He has broken my strength in midcourse;
he has shortened my days.
"O my God," I say, "do not take me away
at the mid-point of my life,
you whose years endure throughout
    all generations."

Long ago you laid the foundation of the earth,
and the heavens are the work of your hands.
They will perish, but you endure;

they will all wear out like a garment.
You change them like clothing, and they
    pass away;
but you are the same, and your years have
    no end.
The children of your servants shall live secure;
their offspring shall be established in your
presence.

Psalm 130   F-12

Out of the depths I cry to you, O LORD.
LORD, hear my voice!
Let your ears be attentive to the voice
    of my supplications!
If you, O LORD, should mark iniquities,
LORD, who could stand?
But there is forgiveness with you,
so that you may be revered.
I wait for the LORD, my soul waits,
and in his word I hope;
my soul waits for the LORD
more than those who watch for the morning,
more than those who watch for the morning.

O Israel, hope in the LORD!
For with the LORD there is steadfast love,
and with him is great power to redeem.
It is he who will redeem Israel
from all its iniquities.

The LORD is my shepherd, I shall not want.
He makes me lie down in green pastures;
he leads me beside still waters; he restores
     my soul.
He leads me in right paths for his name's sake.
Even though I walk through the darkest
     valley,
I fear no evil;
for you are with me;
your rod and your staff – they comfort me.
You prepare a table before me
in the presence of my enemies;
you anoint my head with oil; my cup
     overflows.
Surely goodness and mercy shall follow me
all the days of my life,
and I shall dwell in the house of the LORD
my whole life long.